Convert

How To Turn Website Traffic Into Sales On Autopilot

Jason Drohn

To Chelsey & Sebastian.

For always being the place I call home.

Table of Contents

INTRODUCTION

My name is Jason Drohn, your author. Welcome to *Convert*. This book is all about selling your products and services online. It's based on what I've learned over the past decade plus, selling all types of products and services online in many different niches, working with clients, and doing countless tests to find what works best. It's essentially the last ten plus years of my business life wrapped up in an easy-to-read volume that you can refer to again and again to grow your business.

It really doesn't matter what you're selling as far as the book is concerned. We will discuss concepts and principles that work in any niche. These techniques are independent of whatever niche or industry you're working in.

This book is organized into five major parts and many short chapters.

In Part One, we'll cover sales funnels. A funnel is the process you lead your customers through to get them to purchase from you.

Part Two is all about strategy sessions. These are free, one-on-one calls that are great for selling coaching and other high-ticket services.

In Part Three, we cover webinars in depth. Webinars are a key part of the funnels we build and are an ideal way to sell medium and high-ticket offers.

Part Four covers copywriting. Regardless of what mechanism you're using to sell, it's your words that convince people to buy, so we've devoted this entire section of the book to this critical topic.

Email marketing is one of the best ways to build relationships and make sales to your audience, so we're devoting Part Five to it.

Now, before we get started, I want to cover one thing… The guiding principle I've adopted in my business, and I highly suggest you do the same.

That principle?

To simplify.

Simplify Everything

Everything in your business should be simple.

If a new prospect is asked to jump through hoops before they purchase, it's going to hurt your sales and leads. If a process can be shortened from four steps to two steps, then shorten it.

After marketing for over ten years, I've learned that the simple things are always the ones that make the most money.

If a process is convoluted and has tons of unnecessary steps, it'll bomb.

So, make sure that you're putting together processes in your business that are easy – simplistic even.

That's how this book will be organized: Simply. Step-by-step. Lots of short chapters rather than a few long ones. It's done that way for a reason.

I've taught this stuff tons of times, in many different ways. The format that's seemed to work best is to present the material in short, easy-to-digest chunks. That's why this book has a lot of short chapters rather than a few longer ones.

With that, let's get started.

PART ONE: SALES FUNNELS

Sales Funnels Simplified

Over the past decade, a lot has changed when it comes to selling stuff online - but a lot has remained the same. Sales funnels have gotten a lot more complex thanks to the technology and software we use to deliver targeted, customized messaging, but the overall sales process is similar to what it always has been.

In this section, I'll walk you through our sales funnel process, including all the technology we use, plus how to set up funnels for:

- Affiliate marketing, including landing pages and email autoresponders sequences
- High ticket product and service sales ($1,000 and up)
- Low ticket product sales, both digital products and physical products (under $1,000)

We'll also look at situational sales funnels, where your prospects go through something specific to the action they are currently taking, including:

- Asking for the sale after an opt-in
- Getting the sale after a webinar signup

Plus, we'll talk about advertising success, what that looks like, and what you should be doing next.

Now, what you'll learn in the following pages took me over a decade to figure out, on my own...

I've been selling my own stuff for most of those years and have been working with clients for several years, in every niche you can think of... Photography. Survival. Health & Fitness. Business Development. Dog training. Real Estate. Coaching. Public Speaking. Industrial Manufacturing. Self Help. And many others.

What you will discover in this section is what's worked for us... These are the funnels we always start with.

The metric we look for is simple: We want to double our advertising expense. That's when we know we have a winner on our hands.

So, if we spend $1 on advertising, we want to make $2. If we spend $1,000 on advertising, we want to make $2,000. And..

If we spend $100,000 on advertising, we want to make $200,000!

There are four simple sales funnels that we use depending on what we're selling. And really, the product doesn't matter as much as the price. The price dictates the sales method.

If you want to sell a higher-priced item - like $5,000 coaching or a $10,000 event - the sales process is 'high touch.' There needs to be a higher level of customer interaction to get that sale. The sales process is automated. The pitch is delivered one-on-one.

If you are looking to sell a $97 product, the sales process is 'low touch.' In our world, low touch means 100% automated.

The most important thing is that the product or service is high value. It needs to solve a real problem in your customer's life.

It doesn't matter how good the funnel is if the product is shit. All you're going to get is refund after refund, no matter how much money you make on the front end.

Before we get into sales funnels though, we need to talk about something even more important, "Quickest Path To Cash."

The Quickest Path To Cash

Do you want to make a lot of money online? Selling your own products and services? Amidst all of the shiny objects and wiz-bang product launches?

The answer - Quickest Path To Cash.

One of my college professors taught this way of thinking to me and I use it everyday in my business.

We as entrepreneurs have LOTS of ideas.

There is always something new and flashy hanging out in our peripheral vision...

Shiny object syndrome? Yep, that's what I'm talking about here.

And since the Internet makes it so easy to start a new project or go off on a different tangent, we spend our lives not making ANY money from the PREVIOUS idea.

Always think: "What Can I Do Right Now That Will Get Me Paid Fastest?"

Sometimes, the answer isn't necessarily fun or fast.

- It's that book that's 80% done.
- It's that widget that has everything created except the box labels.

- It's that product that's already done and just needs an order form added to it.

Now, this isn't sexy. It's not push-button riches. That's not how you make money online and sustain it.

You make money by offering something for sale, whether it's a product or service that you own, or something that you sell and can be paid a commission.

Plain and simple.

Getting Sales Online

In order to sell stuff online and successfully architect a profitable sales funnel, there are three pieces of the puzzle:

- **Your Offer** - What you're selling

- **The Follow-up** - Your communication with your prospect once they're in your sales process.

- **Traffic** - The people coming to your website or landing page

The sales funnel is the first thing that you need to set up, even if it's just a standalone sales page.

Next you'll need to quickly add your followup sequence and a supply of traffic to keep sales coming through the door.

You want to make sure you get an ROI (return on investment) from your sales pages, and consistently stoke the fire with new prospects so you can keep growing your business!

When you combine all three - traffic, your offer, and a follow-up process - you get sales!

So, to get this process started, we're going to talk about creating your offer and architecting a sales funnel

Then, we'll get into followup and traffic.

Offers

Before we get crazy into making sales offers and selling stuff, let me describe exactly what an offer is in your prospect's mind.

An offer is anything that requires an action from someone.

- Clicking a video play button is someone accepting an offer.
- Clicking a link in your email message is someone accepting an offer.
- Filling out an opt-in form is someone accepting an offer.
- Purchasing something is someone accepting an offer.

So, whenever you want someone to do something, you're making them an offer.

That includes asking for their email address, phone number, clicking a button or link, or signing up for anything.

And ultimately, making a purchase online.

There is a lot more psychology that goes into it than just putting something for sale online.

You need to convey how your product solves a problem… What features and benefits a customer receives in buying from you… How it'll make their life easier…

There's a lot that goes into it.

First though, let's talk about what you can sell online.

What To Offer

There are lots of things that you can sell online. Some will work in your market. Some won't.

You need to ask yourself what your customers will value AND what you have the ability to create, have created for you, or buy the rights to.

Most people in the digital world think of ebooks and video courses when it comes to products. However, a growing number of business owners are moving toward physical goods, thanks to Amazon's FBA program and sourcing portals like Alibaba.

In the scheme of things, an offer is an offer regardless of how you slice it.

Here are some blanket categories that you can think of selling:

- **Digital products** - ebooks, video courses, membership sites, audio programs
- **Software products** - mobile apps, hosted software (software as a service or SaaS), downloadables, plugins, and extensions
- **Physical products** - shippable, manufactured goods
- **Coaching and Consulting** - group training, individual coaching, in-person consultation
- **Events** – seminars, conferences, workshops, bootcamps, masterminds, paid webinars, online summits
- **Local services** - legal, accounting, financial planning, insurance, contracting, remodeling
- **Affiliate products** – selling someone else's product or service to get a commission

It's ok not to know at this point. You'll need to figure it out before you build out a funnel, but this chapter was written for exploratory reasons as well :0)

Pricing

Pricing is an important component of your product. There are different prices that work better depending on the type of product you're putting out there. You want to make pricing clear in your sales letter. I am going to share with you what is working really well right now as far as pricing with different products.

First, it's advisable that you use a big, orange Add to Cart button, like you can find on Amazon. The button that I use and have a lot of success with can be found all over the Internet. Just do a Google search on it. The Add to Cart button should stick out to your prospect, so they know exactly where to go when they decide they want to buy your product. The Amazon style button works so well because millions of people have purchased off of Amazon before. They know what they're looking for when they want to purchase something, and the button stands out.

The button should link to your shopping cart. Depending on what cart you're using, the button can take you to 1ShoppingCart, ClickBank, JVZoo, InfusionSoft, SamCart, or what have you. We will discuss shopping carts later in the book. Along with your big orange Add to Cart button, it's advisable that you show a higher price crossed out with a lower cost underneath, so people think they are getting a deal, which really they are.

Low end, front ends followed by a higher-priced upsell are working. You can charge $37 for a product initially, which will entice prospects. They buy the $37 product, and then you sell them the $97 product as a one-click up sell. That upsell pricing model works particularly well. On upsells, every increment should be about three times as much in terms of pricing.

If you want to do some sort of live coaching class, you could charge $997, which holds to the times three in pricing. You can also become very profitable when you start building out three, four, or five product chains and just work on upselling.

ClickBank has a Pitchplus program that works really well. Anybody that has a ClickBank vendor account can actually do one-click upsells through Pitch Plus. There is all sorts of documentation available on the site; you can't miss it once you log in to your account. 1ShoppingCart and InfusionSoft both have one-click upsell functions. 1ShoppingCart is easier to set up than InfusionSoft with upsells, as it is with most things.

Pricing is never something that's cast in stone, so it's impossible to say what you can charge for your product.

I've seen 20-page ebooks sell for $1,000 and 20-hour video courses sell for $1. Lots of times, your pricing is really about delivering value and filling a spot in a funnel to move customers and prospects into the next action.

What I mean by that is pretty simple.

The $1,000 ebook is meant less to sell and more to establish value. A customer might look at that and say, "If his ebooks are $1,000 then his coaching at $5,000 is a bargain!"

Likewise, the 20-hour video course at $1 is meant to establish value in the training and catapult a boatload of buyers into action, meaning that there's a great chance that they'll buy an upsell.

In both examples, the offers are more about positioning than anything else.

With that said, here are some general rules about pricing. You might follow this model. You might not. It's totally up to you.

Physical Book

If you're selling a physical book or are planning on selling one, a good price to start is $19.95. If it's for sale on Amazon, a price between $12 and $15 is where you should start.

Ebook

If you're selling just an ebook standalone, on its own website with a sales video or sales page, a good price is $27-37.

If you're selling it as a Kindle ebook or iBook, you can expect between $2.99 and $9.99 usually.

Audio Product

If you are selling just an audio product with an ebook it's going to be $37-97.

This can also be used for audio interviews, tele-conferences, etc. and delivered as an .mp3 file.

Video Course / Membership

If you're doing a video course, with or without mp3 downloads and an ebook, it can be anywhere between $97-997.

Normally, we don't include any live sessions or Q&A calls or any of that in a normal video product. If we want to do something like that, we'll charge more for it (read below!)

Big Box Course

If you want to do a big gun course, like live or a master class course, you can do between $1,000 and $5,000.

This is usually going to be videos, audio sessions, reports, and sometimes some live, weekly classes.

Coaching / Consulting

For the most part, coaching and consulting combine some products like video courses or audio recordings, with some one-on-one or group help.

There aren't any typical prices when it comes to coaching and consulting. You can charge $5,000 a month. $25,000 one-time. $50,000 for the year.

It really just depends on where you want to set your prices and what kind of value you're delivering.

Masterminds

With a mastermind, the value is in the group. The creator is usually more of a moderator than anything and is the person responsible for bringing the group together and leading it.

Masterminds are typically $300 a month to $5,000 a month. There are some that are more expensive and some that are free. It really just depends on the leader and what the overall goals for the group are.

Software

The sweet spot for software, especially when it's hosted and works as a Software as a Service (SaaS) is $97 a month. If the software is more robust (and does the work that an employee would), it can be $297/month to $497/month.

For downloads, plugins, themes, and extensions, typical pricing is between $10 to $70.

For mobile apps, you can expect 99 cents per install to $2.99. In-app purchases can be higher because users are already engrossed in the process. In fact, many of the highest-grossing apps are free and make all their revenue from in-app purchases and advertising within the apps.

The Pitch

Now that we know what we're going to sell, we need to actually make the offer to our prospects. In short, we give them the chance to say, "Yes" or "No."

We're going to talk about a few different sales methods here, both high touch and low touch.

Low-touch sales material like sales videos and sales pages are typically reserved for lower-end products. Higher-touch sales methods are meant to be used for higher-priced offers.

Long-Form Sales Letter

A long-form sales letter is one of those excruciatingly long sales pages, that go on and on forever and sell something.

You know the kind - the ones that take like 30 minutes to read!

Long-Form Sales Letters (LFSLs) used to be the standard way of selling digital products online, but they're largely out of style right now.

They still work, but not when you're sending paid traffic! Paid traffic generally wants to see a video.

Still, you can add a long-form sales letter below your video sales letter or after an exit pop when someone leaves your website. Just make sure to do your tests so that you can be sure that it is in fact increasing conversion! Lots of times, we've found that adding long form sales copy under a sales video actually lowers overall conversion of the sales page and sales copy itself.

Video Sales Letter

A video sales letter (VSL) is the current standard in terms of sales material, as of the last few years.

You'll know them when you see them. Generally, they're a voiceover of a PowerPoint presentation, where the product owner just reads the slides on the screen, slide after slide, recording the process as they go.

They work well, because you force the prospect to both read and listen. The Add To Cart button is often delayed to coincide with the offer, although it doesn't always need to be. For our software products especially, we'll show the Add To Cart button right from the beginning.

VSLs have even been taken a step further recently by using hand drawn animation rather than PowerPoint slides. It's quite expensive per minute of video, but could be worthwhile after your video has been tested extensively.

We will cover long-form sales letters and VSLs in much more detail in Part Four of this book.

Webinars

My #1 recommendation to new product owners is to put together a webinar for their product or service.

Here are some of the benefits of running a sales webinar:

1. They're simple to put on if you have a traffic source
2. Webinars are forgiving, in that you can screw them up and STILL make sales!
3. You can price products from $97 to $25,000 and sell a LOT (the higher the price, the higher-touch the sales process is.)

4. The biggest reason I like them is you can test out different sales angles and see how they work!

If you think one hook will work, test it out! If it does, awesome! You know you just connected with your market.

If it doesn't, rework it and try again!

The main benefit of having a webinar is much more apparent after you run one though.

You see, a normal video sales letter will convert about 1% of the people who watch it... Sometimes, it's a little bit higher.

A good webinar?

A good webinar will convert anywhere between 6% and 51% of the folks on the call!

We've done webinars where we sell a $97 product, and we've converted 51% of the webinar attendees.

We've sold stuff for $2000 and converted 6% of the attendees.

I can tell you, after running hundreds upon hundreds of webinars, there is no better sales medium!

Scriptly has a sales webinar writing tool called the "Webinar Wizard" you can sign up for free here:

http://scriptly.org/webinar-wizard/

The other thing that Scriptly does, as it applies to webinars and selling through virtual events, is write all of your email copy.

Inside Scriptly is both the Webinar Promotion Email Sequence and the Webinar Replay Email Sequence. For those, sign up for a free account here:

http://scriptly.org/video/

See Part Three of this book for much more about webinars.

Strategy Sessions/Sales Calls

Good sales funnels often combine more than one sales medium, to increase the chances of conversion. If someone doesn't want to watch a video, maybe they'll get on a call. You'll have something for everyone.

Strategy sessions are interesting in the sales process because there's an implied benefit to your prospect. They're able to get on a call with you and pick your brain for free.

Some people run these strategy sessions as straight up sales calls with high pressure tactics. I prefer calls that are much more passive.

The way I see it, someone's getting on a call with me. I want to make 100% sure that they're receiving value by way of insight, focus, strategy or process.

If, and only if, there's a way that I can help them get where they're going faster, I'll make an offer. In our case, it's a Done For You sales and marketing solution, so they can concentrate on growing their business.

In some cases, I'll even tell the person that I don't think I'm the right person to help them with their current situation, if that's how I honestly feel. Sometimes turning away a client or referring them to someone else is best for everyone.

Other coaches/consultants/product owners are much more aggressive, and that works for them.

The key to a strategy session is to establish credibility and trust, before making your offer.

You can sell anything you want - coaching, consulting, high-ticket products and services, and services that are a bit more complex (think financial management).

The important thing is to make sure that only qualified folks sign up.

Inside Scriptly, we have a "Strategy Session Autoresponder Sequence" that you can mail out to your list to get call signups.

Visit this page for more info: **http://scriptly.org/video/**

Also, in terms of scheduling sales calls, we've built a tool that'll make the process easy. Just share a link with your prospect, they sign up and fill out a form, and you close them!

Here's a video on that:

 http://timeslots.org/video/

See Part Two of this book for much more about strategy sessions.

Building The Sales Funnel

Now that we've talked about both offers and sales material, it's finally time to talk about sales funnels. Finally, right?

You're going to see why in a minute, but picking the right sales funnel is all about putting your offers together in a way that maximizes sales.

That's how you make money online with your products - you build the funnel that takes cold prospects, warms them up, and ultimately gets them to buy something from you!

We take a bit of a longer tail approach to sales funnels, though. We don't look at the upsell and downsell process and call that a funnel.

We look at ALL of the marketing material and assets, including email lists, email autoresponders, retargeted traffic and offers made weeks and months after the initial sale.

In short, we look at the entire project and engineer a completely unique marketing channel, based on return on investment and customer engagement.

Now, the sales material that you'll present in your funnel depends more on the price of your product than anything else.

Selling stuff online requires that you create desire and match that desire with a price point. Can you sell a $37 ebook from a 1.5-hour webinar? Sure. But why would you?

Another thing to consider is the affiliate payout for your products. People won't promote your product unless they can make what they need to support a few mailings.

And finally, you want to make sure it's profitable to send your own paid traffic to your offers. That's how you scale.

Having the right sales funnel in place is all about making the numbers work!

Here are the four main sales funnels that we employ in our business, day after day.

Affiliate Funnel

The Affiliate Funnel is all about generating leads and moving those leads through a process that gets us affiliate commissions.

The offers are all affiliate offers, network marketing offers, or MLM offers that pay us an affiliate commission or a finder's fee of some kind.

The whole process starts with a landing page with a follow-up series through email. This is the simplest funnel to set up and is perfect if you don't have an offer of your own to market.

The download or 'lead magnet' itself; whether it's a PDF, a video, a set of audios, whatever, is how the whole process gets started.

Inside Scriptly.org, there are quite a few Done For You Affiliate Sequences, including:

- Business Development
- Business Opportunity
- Survival
- Men's "Get Your Ex Back"
- Women's "Get Your Ex Back"
- Dog training
- Women's Health & Weight Loss
- Men's Fitness

- Plus many more niches

Also, when you sign up, you get the Lead Generation campaigns for each of the funnels, so that you can just plug them right into your process!

Here's what the Affiliate Funnel looks like, front to back:

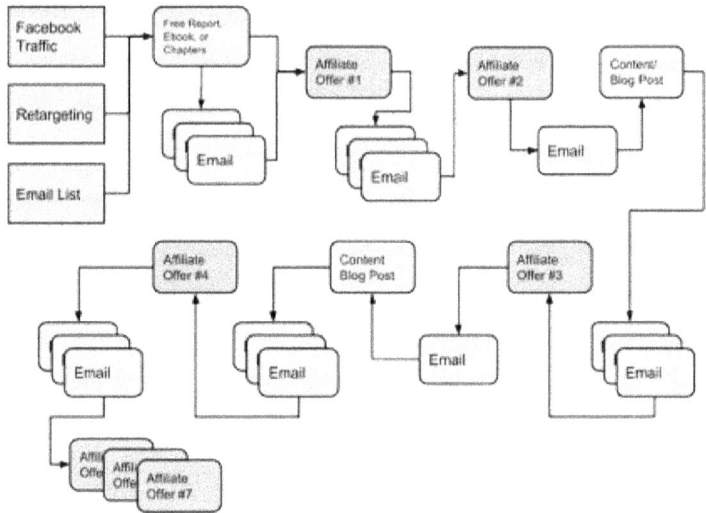

VSL Upsell Funnel

The Ascension Funnel is designed to upsell your buyer through the purchase process.

The first offer, or front end offer, is usually less than $100 and gradually increases in price for two products.

For example, pricing is typically $37, then $97, and then $297. Each upsell is roughly 3X the price of the previous sale.

There is a school of thought here where you offer an extremely discounted front end offer - sometimes $1 or $7 - so that you can get more buyers through the upsell process and maximize profitability.

Through lots of tests over the years, I've had success doing that, and miserable setbacks.

In certain markets like photography and business development, customers regard low price products as low quality. You're better served to offer something at $37 or $67 and then increase the prices of the products in your upsell funnel.

You might get fewer front-end sales, but you'll make more money overall, and get a better ROI on ad spend. If you price too low and your upsell doesn't convert, you end up dropping a bunch of cash on ad budget without ever getting it back.

Here's what the Ascension Funnel looks like:

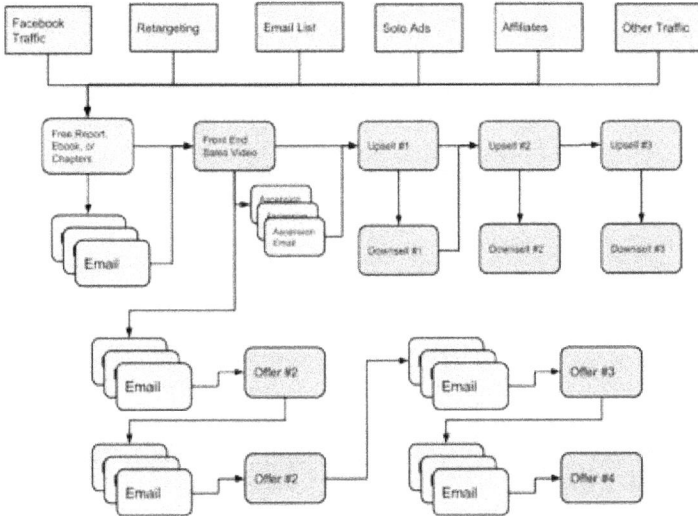

There are a few email sequences inside Scriptly that'll help work your prospects through the process here…

- The Ascension Promo Sequence - It'll help you promote the next item in the sequence that WASN'T purchased. So if someone buys the front end offer and not the upsells, they'll start getting emails about that offer.

- The Flash Sequence - By running a three-day, discounted front-end offer you maximize upsell revenue without sacrificing the perceived value of your front end product.

- The Product Promo Sequence - Mail your list your newest offer, get clicks, and get sales.

The Launch Funnel

Create and popularized by Jeff Walker's Product Launch Formula, the launch funnel should be used with products over $997 and under $1997.

This funnel includes three professionally-done, professionally-written videos that walk prospects through the problem, features, benefits, and case studies of folks who have fixed the problem using the proposed solution (the product).

Executing a product launch is a time-intensive process, between planning, creating, and copywriting.

You can think of it as one long sales presentation, executed through several videos, all leading up to the inevitability of a product launch.

I have seen people run similar launches, without videos though. If you don't have the skill necessary to create the videos, you can do something similar with blog posts and other pieces of content.

Here's what the Launch Funnel looks like:

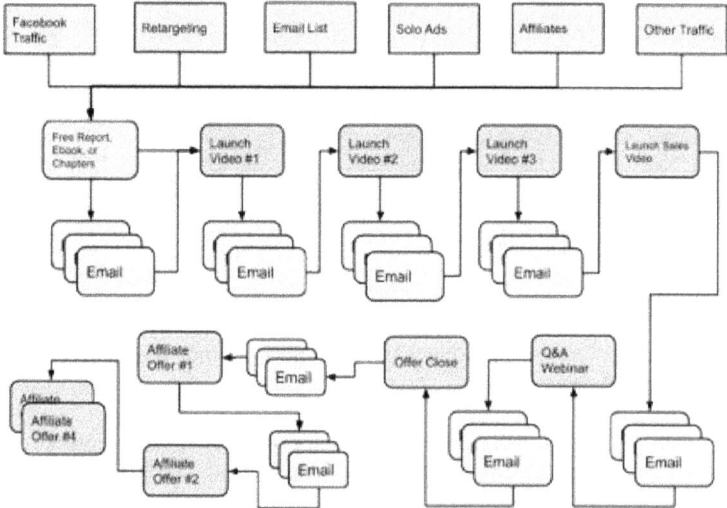

Webinar Funnel

The webinar funnel is entirely based around an event. That event is either a webinar or a teleseminar, and is designed to sell anything from $97 to $20,000.

Prospects sign up for the event and then get reminder emails about when it will occur. The webinar itself is designed specifically to walk through the problem and the product offer within 60 to 90 minutes.

Inside Scriptly, there's a webinar writing tool called the Webinar Wizard. Rather than spending days or weeks writing a webinar, you can get it done in about 15 minutes!

Go to the address below to watch the video:

http://scriptly.org/webinar-wizard/

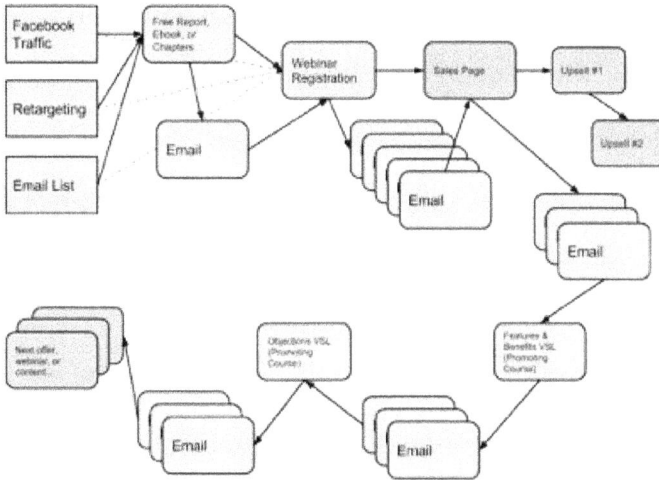

Follow-Up

The follow-up is the marketing series AFTER someone takes action with an offer or opts in to your process.

The better you understand the follow-up process, the more money you are going to make.

In fact, the most profitable way of growing your business online isn't in trying to get new customers.

It's selling more stuff to the folks who already bought from you!

See Part Five on email marketing later in the book for more on how to do this.

PART TWO: STRATEGY SESSIONS

Why Strategy Sessions Convert

Imagine being able to easily sell more of your high-ticket offers.

Imagine looking at your calendar, seeing that you have several calls scheduled with potential clients over the next few days, and knowing that you will be able to sell your offer to a high percentage of them.

Think about your profit margin per sale and imagine several times that amount being deposited into your account in the next week or two as you book these new clients.

This is not a fantasy. It's what this section of the book is all about. We're going to show you a method that is easy to learn and implement that will have you bringing in more high-ticket clients, as well as clients who are more aligned with your style and what you have to offer. It's the best way we've found to make these sales.

Strategy Sessions Defined

Let's define what a strategy session is so we're on the same page. A strategy session is a free, private, one-on-one call with a potential client (or in some cases, customer, student, patient, etc.).

Some people use other names for strategy sessions, such as *consultation calls* or *discovery calls*. Use whatever wording makes sense for your business, and we will stick with *strategy session* for this report.

A strategy session is scheduled in advance and is short in duration, typically 15 to 30 minutes.

The Goal of This Section

The primary purpose of this section is to teach you how to use strategy sessions to sell your high-ticket services and products, such as:

- Coaching
- Consulting
- Therapy and counseling
- Done-for-you services
- Courses
- Masterminds
- Seminars, workshops, boot camps, retreats, etc.

In short, nearly any high-ticket offer can be sold via the strategy session model. Most of the examples above fall into the information marketing industry.

Think about a totally different field, like law. Many attorneys will meet with a potential client for free to discuss whether the person has a case worth pursuing. That is the strategy session model, just usually done in person rather than via a call.

We will often use coaching as an example in this report, so just keep in mind that strategy sessions have much broader uses.

The Power of Strategy Sessions

Many business owners have found the strategy session model to be the best way to sell their high-ticket offers. There are many reasons for this.

It's difficult to sell offers over $1000 or so directly from a sales letter or sales video, no matter how compelling the message is.

It's also difficult to sell one-on-one services like coaching or consulting without first speaking to the potential client, especially if your name is not well-known in your industry. This is actually a good thing for you, since it helps you screen out people who aren't suitable for your program before you start working with them.

Obviously there are exceptions. Someone with a strong, established brand like Tony Robbins can sell their high-ticket offers directly from advertising. However, even companies like that often use some method of selling over the phone.

The Goal of a Strategy Session

A strategy session is not a sales call, although it often results in a sale. The primary purpose of the call is to see whether the potential client is a good fit for what you're offering, and vice versa.

It's especially important to understand the difference between a strategy session and traditional telemarketing-type sales calls, which often use high-pressure sales tactics, are typically done by salespeople who work on commission, and whose main concern is making the sale, regardless of whether the offer is appropriate for a specific client.

Unfortunately, some companies doing that type of selling use the term strategy session, which can give people a bad impression of the term.

(We don't mean to put down traditional phone sales methods, just want to stress that this section is about something completely different.)

We believe that you should have a second purpose for your strategy sessions, to help your prospects as much as possible in the amount of time you spend with them.

Many people are skeptical these days. When they schedule a strategy session with you, some will expect it to be the typical high-pressure sales call. When they realize you're actually having a conversation with them and trying to help them, they will be pleasantly surprised.

As great as it might sound to sell everyone you talk to, that shouldn't be your goal. The odds are high that some of the people on your calls should not become your clients, for various reasons. Some people have unrealistic expectations. Some won't take action on what you teach them. Some will have personality conflicts with you. Some would rather argue than follow your advice. And some are simply looking for something other than what you offer.

It might sound like a paradox, but quite often, the best way to make a sale is to **not** hard sell the prospect. When you speak with ideal prospects, often they will want to buy from you before you bring up the subject.

In some cases, the prospect won't buy your offer for whatever reason, but will be so impressed with the help you gave them that they will refer other clients to you or give you a testimonial.

If you consider yourself to **not** be a natural salesperson, I have great news. The strategy session model is especially suited for you, because it doesn't require you to be the stereotypical pushy salesperson. In fact, people who aren't naturally good at sales often excel at the strategy session model, because it's more about having a conversation and helping people than hard selling them.

This is a skill you can develop. It's not something you have to be born with to

27

get good at doing it.

Regardless of your personality, the more strategy sessions you do, the better you will get at doing them, and the more sales you will make. You will get better at attracting the right prospects to your calls. Both of these factors will lead to a higher percentage of strategy sessions that result in sales.

Other Uses for Strategy Sessions

There are some other good uses for strategy sessions besides screening prospects and making sales.

They can be great for researching your market before you release your high-ticket offer. Once I was creating a high-ticket course and wanted to make sure I covered everything I should, so when I was about halfway through creating the course, I set aside a day to do a dozen strategy sessions.

I told people when they signed up that we could discuss anything they wanted on that particular subject. I spoke with a nice cross section of people and was able to answer almost all their questions. I got several good ideas for things to add to the course that I hadn't thought of. On the calls I didn't mention that I was creating a course and didn't try to sell anything. (Looking back, I probably should have mentioned the course and offered to send them a discount offer on it when it was ready.)

Another great use for strategy sessions is to get a taste of what it's like to do coaching or consulting when you haven't done that work before and might be unsure if it's for you. If you don't enjoy doing a strategy session, you're probably not going to like coaching or consulting very much and should consider creating some other type of offer.

How To Schedule Strategy Sessions

Here are the steps in the process. We will discuss each of them in order after this list:

1. Establish your credibility
2. Schedule the strategy session
3. Form a connection
4. Take the lead
5. Show your value and focus on the results
6. Overcome objections
7. Start the relationship right

Steps 1-2 happen before the call and will be addressed in this chapter. In the next chapter, we will cover steps 3-7, which take place on the call, and step 8, which comes after the call.

Establishing Your Credibility

Before offering strategy sessions, you should start getting yourself known as an expert in your field. This gives you credibility with prospects. If you skip this step, you'll have trouble getting people to sign up for strategy sessions, even though the calls are free. Some will schedule a call but not see you as someone who is worth what you charge for your services. Or they will second guess what you tell them, which makes it difficult if your job is to coach or advise them.

The first half of this is simply getting your name associated with your niche, for example "Sally Smith is a marriage counselor."

The second half is demonstrating that you know what you're talking about. ("Sally Smith is an expert in the field of marriage counseling.")

There are many proven ways of establishing your credibility. Here are some of them:

- Create a blog
- Write a book (printed or ebook or both): For centuries authors have written books to establish themselves as experts, often more than to earn royalties from their books.
- Publish your book for Kindle: Tap into Amazon's huge customer base
- Create an author page on amazon.com and add your blog and Twitter feeds to it
- Guest post on other people's blogs, especially high-traffic sites like the HuffPost and well-known blogs in your niche
- Make thoughtful comments on other people's blogs, especially those which allow you to include a link to your website/blog
- Start an email list and send out quality content to your subscribers
- Write a free report and give it away to get subscribers. Let others in your niche give it away to spread your message
- Write for magazines or trade publications in your niche
- Write reviews for relevant books or other products on amazon.com and use your real name (that you do business with) as the review author

Notice those all have something in common, writing. I realize not everyone likes to write. These tasks can be outsourced. Just make sure the final product that the public sees is high-quality. (If you'd like some help setting this up, visit us at DoneForYou.com.)

We all know how big social media has become. Here are some things you can do to promote yourself there. The best social media sites for you will depend on your niche. Don't feel like you have to have a presence on every social media site, or it could become a full-time job.

For example, sites like Pinterest and Instagram are image-oriented, so if your niche is something visual like art or photography, it might be a good idea to have a presence there. But if you do business consulting or selling insurance, probably not.

- Create a Facebook page for your business and post on it regularly
- Create a LinkedIn page for your business and post on it regularly
- Create a YouTube channel for your business. Make short, relevant videos and post them there. Also post them on your blog and other social media sites
- Join Facebook and LinkedIn groups in your niche and make helpful posts
- Join forums in your niche and make useful posts. Include a link to your site if allowed

Here are some other ways to promote yourself beyond writing and social media:

- Be a guest on podcasts in your niche. Talking about your field of expertise will make you better at doing strategy sessions
- Do as many media appearances (radio, TV, newspapers, etc) as you can
- Attend events in your field. Volunteer to speak and appear on expert panels
- Do interviews in whatever format and media you can, as the interviewer and interviewee
- Get to know other experts in your niche. You can interview each other, refer business to each other, etc.

Scheduling Your Strategy Sessions

Scheduling is important, no matter how much free time you have, because you should start the relationship by stressing that your time (and the other person's) is important and people can't just call you whenever they feel like it to do a strategy session.

So how do you get people to sign up for strategy sessions? First, realize that you can only fit so many of these calls into your schedule, so you should be selective about who gets one. The best way to do this is to make people fill out an application, an online form with some questions they have to answer before they can get on a call with you.

Having an application accomplishes several things. It helps you gather some information before the call about what the prospect is looking for. In some cases this will be enough for you to realize you can't help them, so you can politely cancel the call and save yourself both the time. It shows the prospect you're serious by asking for the information upfront. It helps you prepare for the call by having some idea of what questions or problems the person has. It also weeds out people who aren't serious enough to spend a few minutes filling out the application.

Make it clear to your prospect that you have set aside a specific time period for them (such as 2:00 – 2:30 pm), so if they show up late, they will lose that amount of time. For example, if someone doesn't show up until 2:15, they will get 15 minutes maximum. Be firm on this and don't let people go past the scheduled end of the session, or some people will abuse your time. Stick to the scheduled time slot, even if you have nothing scheduled after it.

Questions to Ask on Your Application

Ultimately it's up to you decide what to ask on your application, based on your business, and this may evolve over time. Here are some suggestions to get you started:

- Basic contact information: name, email address, phone number, Skype name (especially if you are in different countries and don't want to use the phone)

- Tell me about yourself, product, or idea.
- What would be the MOST important criteria for your success as we work together?
- What do you think is holding you back (from reaching your goals, solving your problems, etc.)?

If you're selling business-related services, add questions like these:

- What's your website URL (if you have one)?
- How many people are currently on your email list?
- Current monthly revenue
- Monthly ad budget
- How willing and able are you to invest in growing your business right now?
- At this time, what investment can you make in growing your business?

Technical Aspects of Scheduling Strategy Sessions

Setting up this process online used to require you to use two pieces of software. You needed one to create the application form and another to let people see your available times and schedule your call. There are a number of software products that can create online forms and a bunch of others for scheduling.

We've tried cobbling together various combinations of these products, looking for the best solution. We quickly found that if we have people book a time first, many of them don't bother to fill out the application, either because they're confused or think it's OK to skip that step.

If we have them fill out the application first, many of those who do so don't book a time, for whatever reason.

We found ourselves having to do a lot of manual followup to get everyone signed up properly, and the whole point of this was to have an automated system that prospects could easily use to apply for and schedule a call.

A Software Solution

Unfortunately, there wasn't one software package that did both parts of this process, so we decided to create our own. We now make it available to our clients. It's called TimeSlots, and if you'd like to know more about it, you can watch the video at **timeslots.org/video**.

Boosting Your "Show Up" Rate

Some people will book strategy sessions, then not show up for the call. Here are some things we do to cut down on that.

Once someone schedules a session, follow up with them. Send them a personal email within 24 hours of them scheduling an appointment that takes some interest in them or their business.

For instance, "Thanks for scheduling a call. I checked out your website and I saw that you've got a ton of products - great job!"

Or if your offer isn't business-related, something like, "It sounds like you've made some good progress already. I look forward to helping you reach your fitness goals faster."

Then, always close the email with a question.

For business offers: "Do you have any sales material or webinars that I can go through before our call - so I can familiarize myself with your process?"

For non-business offers: "Which diet plans have you tried so far, and which one gave you the best results?"

In other words, personalize the email so the person can see you're taking an interest in them and their needs, and ask questions that will give you more information you can use to help them on the strategy session.

This dramatically improves the show-up rate.

Conducting Strategy Sessions

Another way to increase attendance rates for your strategy sessions is to call the prospect at the scheduled time, rather than having them call you. Some people just forget or aren't watching the clock, so if you wait for them to call, more of them will miss their appointment.

Form a Connection

When you start the strategy session, put the prospect at ease. Remember that they might be expecting a hard sell call, so when you start asking about their situation and listening to them, that will go a long way towards establishing rapport and building trust.

Show the prospect that you care about them and their problems more than you care about making a sale.

Take the Lead

Once you've formed that connection with your prospect, you must take control of the session. Otherwise there's a danger that it will just start rambling all over the place, your prospect won't get much out of it, they will leave confused or dissatisfied, and you won't make a sale.

Remember, this is a strategy session for a specific purpose, not a couple of friends chatting on the phone. If the client starts to wander off, get them back on track. (If they won't let you do that, that's a sign that they might not be a good client for you.)

You don't have to write a script for your session, but it's good to have an outline of what you want to cover on the call. You can make a standard outline, then modify it a bit for each prospect based on their application. Make sure to answer any questions and address any concerns they listed on their application. Do that before you answer new questions.

Strategy sessions are short by design. The goal is not to answer every question your prospect can dream up, but to help them as much as you can within the allotted time. If they have more questions than you have time to answer, that's a sign that they should be buying your services to work with you further.

Don't let the prospect interview you. Even though buying your service is a form of hiring you, this is not a job interview. Don't let them take control of the call.

Also, don't feel like you have to give the prospect every secret or strategy you know on the call. Give value, but save something for your paying clients.

Keep an eye on the clock during the session. If you sense that the prospect is a good fit for your offer, allow yourself enough time at the end of the call to present the offer, maybe 5-10 minutes. (You'll get a better feel for how much time after doing a few sessions.) Don't get so focused on helping that you run out of time to make the offer properly.

Show Your Value and Focus on the Results

This step builds on the last one. Part of taking control of the session is taking the prospect through a process that shows them the value they will get from your program.

If you can't lead them on the call, how can you coach or consult them in the future?

Remember, you need to establish not just that the prospect can benefit from your service, but that they should get it from you rather than someone else.

This involves painting a picture for them of the results they will get from working with you.

Failing to show your value is one of the top reasons why people won't buy your offer. They might believe that coaching (or whatever the service) is a good idea for them, but not that you're the right person to serve them. This is much like going to a job interview and not being able to show the employer that you are the best person for the job.

Realize that what you're really selling is not your service or product, but the results people will get from it. For example, don't sell them a weight-loss program, sell them the benefits of a trimmer body, better health, higher self-esteem, etc. That's really what people want when they buy something in that niche.

If you have successful clients, you can mention some of their results (while respecting their privacy) as one way of establishing your value.

This is also a good place to mention any testimonials you have from previous clients.

Your goal here is to create excitement. Help the prospect create a vision of their future from the results they will get from working with you. Get them to believe in themselves and that they can achieve their goals.

Overcome Objections

Anytime you are selling something or trying to persuade someone to do something, you can expect objections. These are reasons or excuses for not buying.

Make a list of as many objections as you can think of and come up with replies for each one.

Here are some common ones:

- I can't afford it
- I need to think about it
- I have to talk to my spouse/partner first
- I don't have time

"I can't afford it"

Sometimes this is true, but it's also commonly used by people who don't want to buy.

If you're delivering a service over time, such as a three-month coaching program, one way to address this objection is to offer a payment plan. Instead of paying the full amount upfront, let the client make three monthly payments.

I would not offer a payment plan that lasts longer than it takes to deliver the service. If you offer a six-month payment plan on a three-month program, the client's incentive to keep making payments once the program ends drops dramatically. If they stop paying part way through the program, you have the option of putting future work with them on hold until they catch up with the payments.

PayPal has a program that lets you offer six-month, no-interest financing to your client. The great thing is that you get paid the full amount right away, and the client makes the payments directly to PayPal, so you don't have to deal with it. Check with PayPal for current details, but at this writing the client has to be a US resident and the offer price must be at least $99.

Another price-related objection that you'll probably hear if you're selling anything related to business or making money goes like this: "Give me your service/product for free, then once I make enough money from it, I will pay you for it."

Some people will even phrase that to make it sound like if you say no, your service or product must not be very good and you don't have much confidence in it.

I would never accept that arrangement. It assumes that you and your offer are 100% responsible for the client's success. That's not a premise I would accept. The person who gets in free has less incentive to do their part. Then if they fail because they don't take action, you probably won't get paid, but probably will get blamed.

"I need to think about it"

"I need to think about it" is often true. People have different buying styles based on their personalities, and some of us need more time to make major purchase decisions. Have you ever noticed how some people will do lots of research before buying a $100 item, while others can spend $5000 at the drop of a hat? That's often due to their buying styles, not necessarily how much money they have. Some people need to wait a certain amount of time or look at X number of options before making a decision.

I can identify with this one because this is how I am. If I'm on the client side of a high-ticket strategy session, even if I'm 95% sure I want to buy, I almost always say let me think about it for a day or two. Pressuring me to say yes or no on the spot is going to get you a no for not respecting my need to give the decision some more thought.

The way I would handle this situation is to ask how much time they need to make a decision, then schedule a followup call with them that far in the future. For example, "You need a couple of days, so if I call you at 4 pm Thursday, you'll have a final decision for me?"

I would make that followup call short and sweet. If they say they still haven't decided, that usually means the answer is no, but they don't want to say that directly, so they will keep stalling and hope you eventually get the hint. I would say "OK, you know how to get in touch with me if you decide to take me up on this offer." At that point I wouldn't chase them, since I've already spoken with them twice, and they still haven't given me an answer.

"I need to check with my spouse/partner"

The need to get spousal approval is often a valid objection. I know many people who would get in serious trouble if they spent several thousand dollars on their own without involving their spouse in the decision, so I can't blame them for wanting to check first.

Spousal approval is also commonly used by people who don't want to buy, but have trouble saying no. It's easier for some people to bring up the spouse than reject your offer when talking to you. Some people will even use this as a bargaining tactic, as in "I'm ready to say yes, but my wife might get upset if I spend this much. Can you cut the price so I can get her approval?"

I would handle this one the same way as the person who needs more time. Ask how long they need to check with the spouse and make a decision, then schedule a followup call. It can be hard to tell when this objection is real, since it's such a common situation, so I usually take the person at their word and follow up with them in a few days for an answer.

"I don't have time"

This one doesn't make much sense to me. We assume the person has problems to solve or goals to reach, which is why they booked the strategy session in the first place. Yet they don't have time to work on those things? You can point out that the problems won't solve themselves or goals won't get achieved without taking action, all of which takes time.

The true meaning of this excuse and many other objections is usually one of these things:

- The prospect knows they don't want to buy, but has trouble saying so directly
- You haven't done a good job of establishing your value or explaining your offer. (They know they need help but aren't sure if you're the right person to help them.)
- The prospect is indecisive in general and has trouble making decisions (usually not someone I would want to work with)

The only one of those that you can solve is the second one. You can always get better at establishing your value, explaining your offer and why it's a good fit for the client. You can also get better at screening the prospects via your application.

Keep track of how many people you do strategy sessions with, how many say yes or no to your offer, what objections they have, etc. Over time, you should see your conversion rate go up- that's the percentage of people who book a session and end up buying.

Start the Relationship Right

The final step is to get off to a good start when you have a new, paying client. Many people have buyer's remorse soon after making a major purchase, so part of your job is to reassure them that they made the right decision.

Help your new client achieve some successful result, no matter how small, as quickly as possible. This will build their confidence in themselves and in you.

What's Next

Watch this video about TimeSlots to discover how easy it can be to fill your calendar with strategy sessions and qualified prospects: **timeslots.org/video.**

Strategy sessions are one of the best ways to make high-ticket sales and find the most suitable clients for your business. If you're uncomfortable with selling, don't feel bad. Look at a strategy session as an opportunity to speak with a new person and help them with their problems, rather than a sales call.

The more of these sessions you do, the better you'll get at them. You'll get better at delivering value on the calls, better at signing up the best-qualified prospects for your offers, and ultimately, better at delivering your high-ticket services.

One last thought: if you currently only offer high-ticket services and products, consider creating some low-priced products like courses or ebooks. Adding some of these products to your funnel is a great way to get your name out to the marketplace, show your expertise, and eventually make some high-ticket sales to people who start at the low end of your funnel.

People who have already bought something from you in your niche, no matter how low-priced, are more likely to buy from you again. It's not unusual for someone who buys a $27 ebook or $99 video course to take the plunge into a $2000 workshop or $5000 coaching program, so don't write off the low end of the market.

If you need help designing or building your marketing funnel, or would just like someone else to do that for you, get in touch by scheduling a session with us here:

http://doneforyou.com/book-a-call/

Or watch a workshop presentation we have here:

http://doneforyou.com/workshop

PART THREE – WEBINARS

The Basics

In this section of the book, we're going to go through how to create webinars to convert. These webinars are basically going to serve as sales messages or sales pieces for your prospects.

You're going to be learning some incredible action-oriented strategies that will get people signed up for your webinar, with or without a list. You don't necessarily need a list in order for this to work. If you have one, that's fantastic, and it's going to help you grow more quickly. We're also going to give you some strategies on getting people to attend your webinar. We'll talk about how to make those folks stick around for the close, how to get them to buy your stuff, and how to keep them coming back for more.

Before I knew how to write sales copy, I was making money with webinars. I remember the first webinar that I ever did had 14 people on the call. I was selling a $397 course and we got two buyers. That small test was enough to really get me excited about webinars. That was several years ago.

This section is laid out into a number of short chapters. The chapters are very simple, and they walk you through the front to the back on how to create and scale webinar presentations, and how to sell products, no matter what industry you're in: health and fitness, disaster survival, finance, anything.

The material is designed to help you brainstorm your topic for the webinar, to teach you what works for webinar creation, to produce sign-up pages, to design the webinar itself, to use different thought processes for producing a webinar that works, and to create calls to action, from front to back. So, altogether, the layout is pretty simple.

The first part is discovery.

- Why webinars?
- Why do they work?
- What to talk about on a webinar
- How to plan the right hook so you can get people attending the webinar for valuable information and then leave them wanting more, a.k.a., buying your product

We're also going to talk about promoting your webinar, whether you have a list or you don't.

We're going to talk about what you need: the gear, the software, and items like that.

Then we'll go through setting it all up.

- The technology, whether it's live services or automated services
- The opt-in pages and sign-up pages
- The reminders
- Designing the slideshow for delivery of an excellent presentation

Next, we're going to get into the performance. The performance is going to be the structure of the webinar, the webinar etiquette, different money-getting strategies, and other items that I like to include and test that I have seen work very well for others, or that have worked very well for us. We've run hundreds of webinars over the past few years, and this is really a fantastic topic to explore.

We're also going to talk about the question and answer section, and why it is probably the most important part of your webinar.

I'm going to tell you how to get prepared, and what to get prepared for. If you are like me, you are a little bit introverted and the idea of talking to 50, 100, 250, 500, or even 1,000 people on the other end of the computer is a little bit daunting, so this section will help you prepare for that.
We're going to talk about some top webinar tips and what we've seen work really well. Then, we will get into the follow-up. The follow-up is going to be how to send your replay out, how to format the replay video, how to use surveys in your follow-up, and what kind of stats to expect.

Not many people include stats in their training, and I really wish they would, because seeing someone else's stats, and seeing what the benchmark industry norm is, really helps you figure out if you're doing a good job or not. It gives you a basis for comparison. In a lot of the courses I go through, I don't actually see any of the stats. They don't publish them. They just tell you about the big numbers they are doing. We include some stats, four different price points, and sign-ups for attendees.

We also talk about collecting feedback and how to automate your webinar, so going forward, you don't have to actually be on a computer every single minute of the day.

Next, we will talk about how to scale your webinars, and some different ways to find traffic for them. Even though this isn't a traffic-getting book, we do talk a little about traffic, and how you're going to be able to scale a webinar through traffic.

We'll talk about how to turn one webinar into a business. Generally, a webinar offers one product and we'll talk about upsells, cross-sells, and affiliate products.

Last, I am going to give you some final cautions and tips before we close, and then we'll talk about your next steps, and what you need to complete to grow your webinar business.

Event-Based Sales Triggers

Webinars are interesting because they seem to have a cycle. When I first got into Internet marketing several years ago, webinars were hot. People were selling 2,000 copies of their products with one webinar, and Frank Kern was doing mass-control launch stuff, and Evan Pagan was doing two or three a week.

Then, suddenly, webinars just died down. It was before I had gotten into doing our own webinars. This lull lasted for about a year, with some occasional training stuff, until the summer of 2010, when webinars started picking back up. All of a sudden, there was not a week that went by that there weren't 4 or 5 webinars being run.

Right now, they are starting to dip, because people would sign up and then not show because it was at night, or at an inconvenient time, and they would just go and watch the replay. They wanted the training that the webinar provided, but didn't actually think enough of the webinar to attend. The thing about attendance in a webinar is that is where you will get most of your conversions – right there in the webinar.

So, if you have 1,000 people sign up, and 500 people actually attend, the 50% conversion rate isn't bad, but when you start doing a great many webinars, or a list is mailed to you with people familiar with webinars, you might only get 30 to 35 percent attendee rates. That is why some of the material in this section, as far as offering bonuses and incentivizing people to attend the webinar, is so important.

That is a simple background – webinars are not dead. They are not going away. There are still a ton of markets that webinars are crushing it in, particularly non-IM based. Even so, there are still a lot of Internet marketing webinars that do well.

One of the questions I get asked almost as much as *How do you do a webinar?* is *Why webinars?* The answer is really pretty simple. A webinar is an event. A webinar is something you should, and your prospects should, plan around. So, if you invite someone to a webinar at 9 p.m. on Wednesday or 9 p.m. on a Thursday, then they should make it a point to put in their calendar and actually show up at 9 p.m.

Attendance rates are somewhat dipping and you can always tell at the end of a webinar that the attendance rates tend to dip a little bit. But, the bottom line is that webinars are an event. It is why webinars work; it is why automated webinars work. It is a timed sales message; it is a timed training event.

It is always beneficial, not to call it a webinar, but to call it an event. Evan Pagan has been doing a lot of virtual events, and that is simply a webinar that is timed. People pay more money for them because he is known for doing such live events.

In terms of an event, if you get tickets for a show at the area philharmonic, or tickets for an air show in the summer at some air field, you go, or at least you try to. You put it on the refrigerator, and you say, Saturday at 2 o'clock in the afternoon, I am going to this event. Perhaps, it is a baby shower, or a Stag-and-Drag or something, you go, or you try to. If you don't, then you just don't RSVP. If you have RSVP'd, then you call and say, "I'm not going to be able to make it." So, that is the power of an event. Basically, you plan your whole schedule around an event.

The thing about a webinar as an event is that you get to give people a whole lot more information. Then you close with whatever it is you're selling. You get to go in and basically pick apart the problem that your prospects are having, the people on the other end of this webinar, your attendees, and you get to teach them something.

The nice thing is that your attendees can interact with you. They have a voice. People on webinars use the question box; they use the chat box; you can do polls; there are all kinds of things you can do in a webinar. But, again, people actually have to show up in order to get that information.

Doubtless, you have received one of those free invites to an *Investors' Conference* in the mail? They send you an envelope with an invitation to a free dinner with some financial institute. They want you to invest money in their 401(k) product or to purchase real estate. They bribe you with the dinner or they bribe you with the free event. Those things work because they are free.

You will see a room of 200 to 300 people—it's a captive audience—they are there for a reason. It is all based upon the Law of Reciprocity. If someone feeds you, you're at least going to give them an hour or two of your time in order to listen to them talk. You're not going to be rude, eat dinner and get up and leave. You're going to go, sit down, have a meal, and listen to the speaker line-up.

Those speakers try to hook you in, draw you in, and to get you to invest in their investment choices, buy some real estate course, to get you to buy something. That is why they are giving you free dinner. Webinars are very much the same thing. The only difference is that the event is held online. A lot of time, all you have to do is go, sign up and attend. Marketers use these to create a captive audience.

There are a couple of really awesome things about webinars: you can build a great list; you build a very responsive following; you build your brand; all in one fell swoop.

Here are what webinars let you do: first of all, you schedule an event, and the event can be whenever you want. It can be a weekday or a weeknight. You can invite as many people as you can, depending on the webinar platform that you choose. These have certain tiers, but you can have up to and over 1,000 people at one event. You can speak to them captively for 45 to 60 minutes or so. You are going to be able to train them, and to sell to them, ultimately. You are also going to want to present them with a way of getting more.

The thing about webinars, is—and when I first heard this, I didn't necessarily understand it—with webinars, you may teach them how to do something. Perhaps you are educating on the five foods you shouldn't eat to lose belly fat, or something like that.

You are going to introduce yourself to them; they are going to see you as an expert, an authority; and then you are going to go and solve one of their problems. If the problem is that they want to lose a little weight, then these five foods are something that they should take out of their grocery cart immediately.

If they want more tips and tricks exactly like that, then they have to purchase your product for $37 or $67 or $97 or $1,997. You can do anything with pricing in a webinar. You always want to present them with a way of getting more. If you don't, if you just go in and say these are the five foods that are going to help you lose weight, and if you don't allow them access to something that is going to answer more of their questions, then you are doing a disservice, an injustice, by not allowing them at least an opportunity to get more of whatever it is you have created.

This is something that I didn't necessarily understand the first time that I heard it. I don't like asking people for money, and with the first 10, 15 or 20 webinars that I did, I didn't like the pitch because I didn't like to ask people for money.

Once I got that into my head and ran a few webinars where I didn't ask them to buy anything, it made sense. All of sudden, everyone was asking where they could get more information, and I didn't really have anything. I'm not selling anything in this call, but if you ask… The bottom line is people want more from you.

Webinars also let you answer questions, so answering questions is huge. It lets you get a feel for the market. It lets you get a feel for the people on your list, and for the people who are going to be buying your product.

Getting to know them better, actually establishing and building relationships with those people, means everything. Those people are going to be with you forever. If they bought one thing from you, and if you don't make them mad, they are probably going to buy more. That's the idea.

If you get a buyer, they are worth 4 to 5 times more than just a prospect. They have already told you that they want to buy from you; they've raised their hands up; they like your stuff; they like your message; they like your training; and they want more.

People sign up for webinars for a variety of reasons. First of all, they like you. People don't necessarily do anything you ask them to unless they like you. *Know*, *Like* and *Trust*—that whole scenario.

So, in order for them to follow you, buy from you, actually do something that you ask them to do, they have to like you. Online, it is a little more difficult because there is no body language, there is no facial expression, there is no verbal word-to-word. What people do is they end up relying on social media, websites, or on your email copy writing. They try to get a feel for who you are based on all these things that you create.

Bottom line is people will sign up for a webinar because they like you. They will also sign up because they want to learn more from you, and this is where the signup page really starts. The name of the webinar, the title, what you're going to be going through on the webinar—if all of that is relevant to the prospect, then they are going to sign up.

They will also sign up for the webinar if they like what you are going to be talking about. Even if they don't necessarily have a problem that needs to be fixed, if they enjoy that particular topic, they will sign up.

They will also sign up if they want more information about whatever that topic is going to be. These are all the reasons why people sign up. They don't sign up to buy from you. They don't sign up because they want to be pitched.

They sign up because they want to learn. They want to be educated. They want more information about something. So, in order for you to uphold that part of the deal, that part of the bargain, then you are going to have to deliver. You are going to have to prove that the information, and the time that they spent with you, has been valuable. The only way to do that is to educate.

There is always a carrot! Something they want—and it isn't your product. People don't sign up on a webinar for your product. I have talked to so many businesses that do a webinar and say, "Hey! How are you? I am So-and-So from Such-and-Such, and what I'd like to do today is talk to you about our product, or our service. Our service can handle this-and-that, and it can do this-for-you and that-for-you and it is only $497. All you have to do is click the button below."

There is a problem with that. There wasn't any value. There was no value delivered. It has basically broken every piece of the trust built up to this point. So, that is why you always have to have a carrot. You always must have something of value that you're going to be able to teach somebody, so that they naturally come to the conclusion that they want to buy from you.

I have worked for a lot of people who think that as soon as someone shows up for the webinar, they are allowed to start pitching, and that is totally not the case. In most cases, these prospects don't know you. They don't care about what you are offering. They will leave the webinar feeling as though you have wasted their time. That is the bottom line.

It's terribly brand-damaging when you treat your prospects and your webinar attendees like one great big walking wallet, particularly when you start getting into 4- or 5- or 10-thousand dollar products, or memberships, and the like. So, you need to deliver value first. You need to walk through a typical problem and deliver a solution. You talk about how your product helps solve that problem.

One of the things that I really like to do on a webinar is walk through and say, "This is how you start a business. In starting a business, you need to do A, B, C, D, E, F, G. You need to all of these things, or you can buy my product, and it will actually cut that time. What used to take you three months, now it will take you three days." So, the product needs to solve a problem.

We try to pack as much volume into our webinars as possible. We try to make sure that the hour, hour-and-a-half, or two hours that they spend on that webinar with us is the best two hours of their week, their month, their year.

We try to make sure that they can leave with enough understanding and enough information that they can go and solve some of their problems without having to do anything extra. Yes, we want them to buy our product, but the bottom line is we want people to come back to us when they start having issues in the future.

Webinars can be used to sell stuff at any price level. Less than $100 is pretty easy. Between $100 and $1,000 is a little bit more difficult, but still relatively easy. You are still going to get 10 to 14% conversions as long as you follow the webinar blueprint that we have in this book.

Between $1,000 and $2,000 is more difficult, especially in this business Internet market. There are a lot of people who had $2,000 products and they either did not deliver on them, or the information wasn't as good as it should have been, and the price has really been driven down tremendously.

Above $2,000 is difficult to sell through a webinar with one interaction. You really haven't had a chance to bond with the prospects at all, especially not to ask for $2,000. It is difficult, but there are some advanced techniques that make that easier. We'll be talking about those in a later chapter.

You can sell anything on webinars! You can sell:

- Windows
- Printing services
- Local marketing
- Physical products
- Digital products
- Coaching and consultation
- Vacation packages
- Seminars
- …anything!

You name it—you can sell it on a webinar. That is the beauty of it.

Last, but not least, webinars convert better than sales letters—bottom line. I've talked to friends who have really great information product businesses, and they solely use webinars as a substitute for sales letters, because webinars will convert at anywhere from 25 and 30% of their price point, which was $67. Sales letters converted 4%.

That is why they use webinars for everything. They are also very easy to set up; they are easy to brainstorm; they are easy to walk-through; and they are easy to ask for a close. You should have success on your first try.

If you have more than 15 or 20 people on your first webinar, you should have success on your first try. You hardly need any technology. You can use the microphone on your laptop, and there are 30-day trials of webinar services. It is easy to pull off.

Webinars are really very easy to put together and pull off as long as you follow the formula that we're going to outline in the rest of this section.

Finding The Right Topic

Choosing the topic for your webinar is your first big hurdle.

There are a couple of questions that you need to ask yourself before you get started:

- What do I talk about for 45 minutes? What is it that you can just riff on for 30-45 minutes that is going to be interesting and somewhat entertaining and educational to the people who are showing up?

- What will people be interested in knowing? What is the market that your product is in? What are people going to actually spend an hour taking in?

- What is normal on a webinar? Just ask yourself, if you have been on any webinars, and I am assuming you have, what do people in your market generally talk about? Because if you have seen the same webinar happen a few different times, then that topic resonates with an audience.

- What is the typical sequence of events? In those webinars, how does the webinar presenter actually put together the webinar itself?

- What will keep people on until the end?

These are a few of the things you have to think about before putting your own webinar together. If you can figure out what would keep you until the end of a webinar, chances are your prospects are going to be incentivized by that same thing.

Typically, webinars go like this:

Minutes 0-5:

These minutes are really pretty simple. Hey, where are you from? Can everybody hear me okay? Questions and answers like a pregame.

Generally, when we start up a webinar, we say, "Hey, this is Jason Drohn. Thanks so much for joining us on this webinar tonight. We'll get started in about 3 or 4 minutes. Let's go through and make sure that everyone is online and signed up, but until then, in the question box, please say yes or yay or whatever. Just let me know that you can hear me okay, because every once in a while, the audio goes out. Okay, cool. Where is everybody from? A lot of times, we get people from the other side of the world, and they actually had to wake up or set their alarm to get up and listen to us talk. So, I like to give a quick shout-out to let me know where everyone is from? Paris, Georgia, Tennessee, Texas, California? Alright, cool. Awesome. So, we'll just wait a couple more minutes…? Okay, so tonight, we're going to talk about…"

Minutes 5-15:

You introduce your webinar and you introduce yourself. You talk about you. My name is _____. This is my background. This is my company. I tend to shorten that up a little bit, because I tend to deliver more content. 5 to 15 minutes is normal.

"Hi, my name is Jason Drohn. I used to be a Pepsi truck driver. I always thought I was more. I was enchanted by this technology thing, enchanted by the internet, blah, blah, blah…"

So, that's how I kick off my little spiel. It does a couple of things. It bonds you to the audience a little bit. It also lets people know what your background is, and where you are from. Some people really like to dig into your background, "How long has it been since…?" You see a lot of the questions.

Minutes 15-45:

Deliver value. This is your content piece. This is where you answer what your topic is, and you give those *A-Ha* moments. There need to be *A-Ha* moments. You need that light to go on with the people in the audience. If that light goes on, they are inches away from buying something from you.

Minutes 45-55:

You introduce the product; you walk through the features and benefits; you show some images of the product; and maybe share some testimonials.

Minutes 55-60:

Price and Call to Action. "For only $97, you can get instant access to download this. All you have to do is go to domainname.com/webinar. This will be a short page, and it will have all the pieces of the product. You will be able to click the *Add to Cart* button and purchase."

Minutes 60-90:

Question and Answer. The question and answer section is the most important section in your webinar because you're going to be able to consistently bring people back to the product. Does your product cover this? Yes, it does. All you have to do is go to domainname.com/webinar and purchase. That's how we like to maneuver through the question and answer. Be sure to put that order page address on your slide.

The Q&A piece is where you are going to get most of your sales. When you actually do that initial Call to Action, you're going to get 5 to 6% of people taking you up on your offer. 20 to 25%, depending on your price point, are going to take you up by the Question and Answer. The question and answer piece is huge.

We're going to be going through each of these parts in greater detail, but the big one is the Deliver Value piece. By delivering value, it's always easiest to start up with the "Five Things You Need to Know about _____" title or some kind of *list* topic.

It's very, very easy to put together. If you have a product in the market, you probably already have a report that you can use to sum up that content for this sort of a topic. So, for example:

- 5 foods you should be eating to lose belly fat
- 7 things you need to do to be prepared for the end of the world
- 3 proven methods of getting your girlfriend back
- #1 way to save money on your electricity bill
- 4 things you need to know before buying new windows

These little benefit-laden statements are perfect topics, and also perfect headlines for your webinar. The list-style topic is great, because it lets you do two things: it tells the prospect what they're going to learn if they sign up; and, it also gives you a pretty compelling title.

I have found that a very well-structured webinar, like these list-style webinars, are the best received, and work the best. You give snippets of information and training without revealing the whole, under-the-hood system. If you have a product on how to lose weight, then you can actually go through and deliver the five foods you should be eating to lose belly fat. Then you may say, if you like this stuff, and if you want more, all you have to do is go to domain.com/webinar and purchase our course.

All you will need to come up with is about 30 minutes of content. Bottom line. The first 5 minutes are just general, "Hey, how are you? Can everybody hear me okay?" A little bit of banter back and forth. You can even ask some folks questions, or tell jokes, or do whatever. You have 5 to 10 minutes to introduce yourself, talk for 30 minutes about the topic itself, and then you start closing them.

There are other ways of picking a topic. I found that the best thing to do is start out with the list-style webinar and then, ask! So, you start off with the "5 Things About..." or "7 Deadly Things..." and when you start building your list, or you already have a list, you ask your people what they want to learn more about. Let them tell you what they want to know more about, or what they want changed. I survey my folks a ton, and it is fantastic.

The next topic is thrown in here because it's worthwhile to think about it when planning your webinar. It's known as Pain Points. The first 15 minutes of the call, while you're talking about yourself, and in the first few minutes of the delivered content phase, you should be focused on a Pain Point: something that irks the people in the audience, something that bothers them, something that drives them crazy, something that they want to fix, something they want to solve, and the only way to solve it is with your product.

The reason I'm saying that is because I've seen webinars in the past that didn't necessarily have a very defined Pain Point, and conversions were always lower because they never actually rubbed it in.

So, a couple of things to ask yourself when thinking about a Pain Point are: Why are prospects on the call? Why are people giving you an hour of their day? What is it to solve? Why are they giving you their time? They are giving you not only time on the webinar, but also time reading your emails, time signing up, time watching the replay. They are giving you their time for some reason. It's not necessarily because they like you, or they want to hear your voice, or any of that. They are giving you their time because there's a benefit, an implied benefit. What are you solving?

That's the Pain Point that we really want to figure out and rub in. By rubbing it in, we're going to continue bringing it up, to say how you struggled through it, and how you eventually came to solve that Pain Point. They're trying to solve something in their life, just like you when you first started trying. What is that? Make sure to aggravate that Pain Point, and then start to provide some answers to that Pain Point in the content piece of your webinar. Then, the ultimate answer is for them to buy and consume your product.

Here is an example:

"I was just like you. I had my fiancé walk out on me because I was working too much and not paying enough attention to her... But her leaving was a wake-up call for me. I regretted every minute of the three months we were apart... And I found these three things that worked... I had a few of my buddies try them out after they broke up and almost every single one of them had great success… So, I want to share these with you today—hopefully they work as well for you as it did for me…"

I'm just grinding that Pain Point and now, this introduces the content piece of the call. We will talk more about that later.

The Right Hook

In this chapter, we're going to talking about the right hook, and how picking the right hook is going to be crucial to the success of your webinar. Getting the right hook, the right reason for people wanting to sign up, is as much an art as it is a science.

If your hook isn't right, you won't have nearly as many people signed up for your webinar as you expected. The reason is because there is a disconnect. There is a disconnect between why the people think they're there, and what you're asking them to do. It might be the wrong audience or it might be the wrong hook.

That's something that you need to think about. Who is coming to your webinar Sign-Up Page? Who do you want actually to be on your webinar? What is the hook and how are you actually going to get them there? If your hook is right, you're going to be beating them off with a stick. If you have a good hook in the right audience, then people are going to be signing up in droves.

This goes back to the Pain Points. Why should people care? What's in it for them? Bottom line—if you can't answer: What's in it for them? What's in it for the people that you're trying to sign up to your webinar? —then you need to rethink the topic.

People attend events, or do anything for that matter, because of two reasons: to avoid pain or to have pleasure. People move twice as fast to avoid pain than to have pleasure. That's why people are signing up for your webinar. They're trying to avoid the pain in their life. They are trying to live their life better, easier, faster, richer, skinnier—that's why people are signing up for your webinar. They think you're going to give them some secret that's going to help them in their lives. You should make the hour they spend on the line with you worthwhile.

In your webinar, you need to give them something that they can use immediately to improve their life. You also should help them solve something that they're having a problem with.

Bottom line—you need to give *A-Ha* moments in your webinar. If you give *A-Ha* moments, you're going to sell a lot of product. If you don't, if you just pepper them with information that that they already know, that they've heard before, they're going to sign off and forget about you. They're going to unsubscribe from your email list and that's it.

You give them *A-Ha* moments to actually open their mind up a little bit, and teach them something that other people aren't teaching, or something that is working in your life, or how it worked, or why, or the process behind why it worked, then they're going to purchase your stuff and recognize you as an expert. Seriously, let them see you as an expert.

The Internet is about building a brand, a personal brand, especially in this world. People would rather buy from a person than a company. The people on the webinar are there, not because you represent a company, but because you're you, and because they can learn from you. They can take what you know, and apply it to their life.

You need to figure out what their Pain Points are. Figure out why it is that they are even entertaining the idea of signing up for a webinar. What is it you can answer for them that they can't find elsewhere, or that they can't find without seriously, seriously looking?

On our webinars, the right hook is something easily achievable. It is not how to make $17,000 in the next 3 minutes. It's nothing like that. It's— How to Make $100 a Day, or How to Use Your Blog to Attract Customers, or How to Sell More Products Online.

We sell businesses on how to do Internet marketing. We go through Internet marketing, give a bunch of *A-Ha* moments, and then at the end, we have them sign up for a strategy call. That's the entire idea of the webinar itself, and the hook is, every business wants to know how to sell more online.

It's like the Great Unseen—like The Great Oz. People look at it like it's some foreign being, and it's not. But, the problem is, they don't have the time, the willpower, or the cash to pay somebody who actually knows what they're doing to go figure it out for them. So, business owners sign up for the webinar on how to sell more stuff online, and they learn about some stuff, and learn that it is easier for you to go do it for them. So, they say, you should just go do it for us. Then, we happily sell those services to them!

That's the idea behind the right hook. You want to match up what it is you're selling with your audience, and give them some bridge in the middle that actually delivers some value, and then also sells more of whatever it is you just delivered.

Promoting Your Webinar

Promotion tips are going to be delivered in two flavors. First, if you have a list—you have an audience that you can leverage. Second, if you don't have a list. We have some tips for both.

In webinars, I've got more of a Ready, Fire, Aim approach. I always figure out how to promote the webinar before I actually do the webinar presentation. This is kind of one of my things. I always go out and line up promotional partners, figure out the different steps to take in order to get the webinar out there before I even write the webinar. I don't actually write the 20 to 30 slides for the webinar until a couple hours before it takes place. I advise you to do a little bit more than that planning-wise—I have done hundreds of these and I know the format pretty well.

There are a ton of ways to promote a webinar, and they depend on your reach. If you have a list, then it's going to be a little bit easier to get folks on the call. If you don't have a list, it's going to be a little bit more difficult. Either way, we're going to give you some strategies that are going to work for you. We're also going to give some general overarching strategies to everyone, if you have a list or not.

If you have a list, email them three times, inviting them to sign up for your webinar. With our list, we'll set aside three days to email for the webinar. We'll email two days before the webinar, the day before the webinar, and then the day of the webinar. Each email should be different with different content. You point them to sign up to the same URL. The email will include some bullets about what you're going to be talking about, and have the sign-up link in that email two or three times. I usually try to close the email by telling them that, in order to get the replay, the video recording of the webinar, they've got to sign up. Basically, only that list will be mailed the replay link.

Here's an example of an email that we have for one of our webinars, a Day One email, with an example of the kind of the formatting. I have bracketed off some items for you to make it easy.

The title of the webinar is How to Be a Local Marketer, and the subject of this email is Big Money Helping Businesses.

Hi,

I'll make this quick...

On Wednesday at 9 pm EST I've got a very special presentation coming up for you here, all about how to be a local marketer:
[signup page]

Normally, I don't get excited about these kinds of things - but this is different.

You've been asking me to put on a presentation like this for quite a while, and I finally decided to do it.

During the webinar, you'll discover:
* benefit 1
* benefit 2
* benefit 3
* benefit 4
* Plus much more!

All you have to do is register for this free webinar, and you'll be emailed a link to join in!

[signup link]

I assure you, it'll be well worth your time!

Jason Drohn

P.S. Spots for these webinars ALWAYS go quick, so make sure you sign up.

Reserve your spot- sign up here:

[signup link]

The second email doesn't need to be nearly as long. You can just reinforce some of the high points of the former one. The third email is very short: "Hey, the webinar is going on tonight. Here's what you can be learning. Here's the link."

If you don't have a list, make sure to post your webinar link on Facebook, LinkedIn, Twitter—wherever you have a social media presence.

I have also really come to love press releases, and you can use a few different services for press releases. One notable one is webwire.com. The other is PRweb.com. Both are paid services, but you get great distribution. They are going to make sure that your article is sent out to some really big media outlets with a lot of people reading that article, so you should be able to build your webinar list.

Alternately, you can set up an affiliate program, and have other people mail to your webinar. There are different ways to do this, and perhaps the easiest way is to use 1shoppingcart.com. The second easiest is probably ClickBank.com. The goal is to get other people to promote your webinar for you, and this will be seen when we start talking about scaling—taking a webinar that converts and then scaling up to be a multimillion dollar business.

Webinars are a pretty short-term thing. You have about a week to promote—perhaps three to four days. There are paid strategies, which I see a lot of people doing now, such as Facebook ads, pay-per-click ads, or Adwords, setting up advertising with the CPA network, or banner ads, such as using sitescout.com and buysellads.com. We'll talk more about these later in this section. These platforms allow you to get traffic and signups for your webinar.

The bad thing is, if you're like me, you bootstrap your success. So, you do a webinar that works and converts, and then you figure out the numbers. You make $2 per person who signs up, and as long as you spend less than $2 to get somebody on a webinar, then you can make money. That's how I gauge a lot of webinar growth, and how I will teach you to do it later on.

Either way, if you have a list, mail that list three times to promote your webinar. If you don't have a list, do the social media syndication. Either way, with a list or with no list, do press releases. Press releases are pretty hot right now. They rank really well in Google, and they're going to get you some great exposure.

What You'll Need

In this chapter, we are going to talk about what you need to run a successful webinar, the software and the hardware that you will need to have access to.

You will need:

- Software for running the webinar itself
- Software for formatting the presentation
- Microphone
- Camera

The last one is optional. You don't necessarily have to do any video, but some people like to, because they feel they perform better on video. In fact, it is probably better if you don't—this is not normally how webinars are done.

There are two brands of live webinar software which we have used in the past:

- GoToWebinar.com – this tends to be the default standard. It used to be more economical, but not as much anymore. You used to be able to get a 1,000-participant package for $100 a month. Now, it costs $249 a month for 500 people. So, you may need to scale as you see fit.

- WebinarJam – this is a newer service but has revolutionized the industry in terms of webinars. One thing I don't like about it though is it's built on the back of Youtube... Meaning, you're relying on Youtube servers, Youtube permissions and your attendees have to jump through hoops to get into your presentation. It's cheaper than GoToWebinar though.

For automated or recorded webinars, there are many options. Every Internet marketer has a solution for recorded or automated webinars. We have used EverWebinar.com and StealthSeminar.com.

There are drawbacks to each of them. They don't necessarily send out the reminder emails that they should, but you can bridge that gap a little bit by having the correct email marketing platform, and tying it all together.

We're going to be going through some of the intricacies of these in a later chapter when we get into some of the more automated pieces of software.

For presentation software itself: PowerPoint and Keynote. Presentations do not need to be elaborate. Some are more image-oriented; some are more text-oriented. We are more text-oriented. Keynote is for Mac users. It is a fine piece of software for putting together presentations, but most of what we do is in PowerPoint.

If you're using Windows and don't want to pay for PowerPoint, the free OpenOffice suite from openoffice.org includes a PowerPoint clone. Google Drive also works very well.

For audio requirements, the onboard mic is probably fine. Most webinars that you hear, or that you attend, are using the onboard mic. They don't necessarily have a offboard mic—something that you plug in. However, if they do, it is usually like a Blue Yeti or an Audiotechnica AT2020. I actually have the Audiotechnica, and it works just fine. Right now, I'm just on a headset mic with a boom mic. The Blue Yeti or the Audiotechnica are about $100 to $120 each. For webinars, the onboard mic is easier.

For video requirements, if you're going to use video in your webinar, the onboard webcam is fine. If you don't have one, the Logitech C920 works really well, or the Logitech Pro 9000, which is actually the version before the C920.

You probably don't need a webcam. It's really not even recommended, but some people like to display themselves. That's just a personal preference. I would not recommend that webinars have a video, because it takes more bandwidth. It may hang up or freeze, but you can always test adding video and see how it goes.

Webinar Setup

In this chapter, we'll walk through the webinar setup.

The first thing we're going to cover will be the technology used in running webinars. There are live services and automated services.

We'll also walk through some ideas on how to get the most signups, get the best conversion possible for your webinar signup page, reminders and why they're important, and how you set up the reminders if you are using automated services—most live services do it pretty well—and we are also going to talk about putting together the PowerPoint itself.

Like I said earlier, I'm a little bit more *Ready, Fire, Aim* when it comes to this stuff. I tend to plan and schedule the webinar before I actually put together a PowerPoint. You may or may not be that way, but we're going to walk through the PowerPoint, and the different things you need to cover in it.

From there, we're going to get into the presentation itself, or the performance.

Live or Automated?

Let's talk about live or automated webinar platforms.

Some folks ask, What is the platform? The platform is the software you use for the webinar itself. It is all hosted. You don't need to have anything on your servers, or any of that other stuff, which is nice. It is considered a software as a service. Basically, you pay for a license or a user account, and you have the ability to run webinars from it.

Let's start by talking about the Live versus Automated conundrum.

Some people think live is better. Some people think automated is better. We have our own viewpoints, which we're going to discuss in this chapter.

When you are running a live webinar, it is live. It is a true event. You give up an hour or two of your time, and the 100 to 200 people attending the webinar give up an hour or two of their time to listen to you talk or to listen to you present and educate them.

That's the thing about live—people can ask questions, and you can answer those questions, live, and there isn't an issue when it comes to response.

You also get to gauge the feedback of the audience. Some audiences just aren't necessarily as skilled as other audiences. A lot of times, you end up getting somebody to mail for you and your webinar, or an affiliate mails for your webinar, or you get traffic from one source, say Facebook, and they just don't necessarily have that foundation for what it is you're talking about. They are interested in it, they want to learn more, but they might be a little bit behind. Think about when students from 8 or 10 different grade schools all go to high school, the high school has to start at a very foundational level, in order to build all the students, from all these different places, up through the ranks.

When you're running a live webinar, you can tell that. It is just like a teacher in the classroom who is able to judge, test, quiz, and see how well-versed the students are in the subject matter that they're trying to teach.

You can't do that with automated webinars because you're not there. The automation just happens; the webinar just goes, and you have no idea what level that audience is at.

Also, when you run live, you present to a crowd, which can help with energy. Energy is one of those weird things. I'm not real big into the cosmic energy of the universe, but the same time, I do know that when you're listening to somebody speak who doesn't have a lot of energy, you tend not to respond with a lot of energy.

Presenting to a live crowd, when people are actually asking questions, giving you feedback, giving a thumbs-up or thumbs-down, and all that stuff, on a webinar, then your energy level goes up, because your audience has a certain energy level. Again, automated webinars don't allow that, because it's basically just a recorded video.

A drawback of live webinars is that you have to block out two hours per day for every webinar you run. Some people can run around two to three webinars a day, on different topics, or the same topic, and you can tell. When they're in their fourth or fifth hour of running webinars, you can tell. It's draining. It's an intensive process if you plan on repeating it.

If you do a webinar that works really well, and your plan is to continue running live webinars, what can happen is the *genuineness* can leave your voice after the fourth, fifth, sixth, or twentieth webinar, because it is so rehearsed. Many times, the first few times will be your best for conversions and it will trail off from there. You will have to be a very good actor, once you are practiced, to maintain that flair and that energy, that rawness. You just don't get that when you run webinars 20 or 30 times.

Now we'll discuss the pros and cons of automated webinars. First of all, it is automated, so it is an Internet marketer's dream. It is passive income. Folks sign up, go through this webinar, and you make money. You don't have to be there—it is a system that just works. That is a huge benefit of automated webinars. You don't have to be in front of the computer to make money. You can travel, you can step away from your computer, your house, your office, and that webinar runs when you tell it to run. People attend it like it's a live webinar.

A downside is you cannot see the audience. You can't interact with them. You can't feel their energy. Nor can you tailor the webinar. If a certain group of the audience does not understand, you are unable to back it up a couple steps, and tailor that presentation to them, which ultimately is a benefit of the live webinar.

Another drawback is that you cannot answer all the questions that show up on the webinar. If you have 500 people on the webinar, and a good portion of them have questions, you can't go through and answer them, so you are unable to focus your message. Most of your sales will come through the question and answer section. In order to run a successful automated webinar, you need to make sure that the questions answered are, largely, part of the bigger group and some of the most common questions.

There is also a certain amount of risk to automated webinars. What if it doesn't play? What if it just doesn't start? One time, we had 2,400 people signed up for an automated webinar. I was pulling my hair out leading up to the automated webinar, because what if it doesn't start? What if it doesn't go off? All these people are going to have to reschedule or do something else. It could be a nightmare.

But, most of all, some people feel cheated. They feel that they were told it was going to be a live webinar, and it's actually a replay.

Nowhere in your marketing material should you ever say it is a live webinar if it is not. People are not dumb. But, some people, when they hear it is a webinar, assume that it will be live. That assumption is sometimes enough to throw off their idea of what it is you are actually doing.

In one of the courses that we still run successfully, we have a $97 weekly training. I ran this coaching session eight or nine times every Wednesday night. I ended choosing one particular replay that had the most general questions that applied to all audiences, and I just automated that.

Although it did free up some time, there were some people that felt cheated. They sent in support tickets saying that they felt they wasted their time, because it was automated. But it wasn't! I responded to every single one of them personally and said, "Look, I ran this webinar so many times, that I knew all the questions asked and how to answer them, so I automated this one webinar that had the best questions. Then I followed through, and if the question isn't answered in the course, then I will answer that question in an email, and actually get some more questions that way."

The response was fine for the people that called me out on it, but just to let you know, some people do feel cheated when they find out that it is an automated webinar.

We have gone through a little bit of the software platforms earlier, but I really wanted to go through them in more detail..

For live software, GoToWebinar.com is the trusted authority. It is a little expensive, with the price I that we talked about earlier. It used to be $97 for the big package, now it is $499 a month, though you can get a 100-attendee package for $109 a month. It is still worth it. It works all the time. It does what you expect it to and it has been around forever. There are no bugs in the software.

What I would do is start with the cheapest package and once you bump past the 100 normal attendees, then go to the 500 attendees and then ultimately, the big package. If you can afford an annual plan, that would be fantastic. You save quite a bit of money.

So, just to walk through GoToWebinar, start at the My Meetings page. From there, you can Host a Meeting, Schedule a Meeting, or simply Join a Meeting. (For some reason, GoToWebinar likes to refer to a webinar as a meeting- don't let that confuse you.)

Under My Webinars, you will see all your scheduled meetings.

Scheduling a webinar is easy: Enter a webinar name, which is going to be your signup page title. Type your description, which is going to be the content and the body of the signup page, the date and time of the webinar, and the audio preferences—you will using VoIP. Most of this is all perfect for what you you're going to need. Click Save and Continue and go through the rest of the setup options.

When you reach the Branding page, I usually don't change anything here. You can test some the different themes. I usually just do Basic.

In the "When attendees arrive, show them this welcome message" field, usually I say something like, "We're going to start right on time, so make sure you grab pen and paper, and are ready to get started."

There are several fields you can choose to collect on the Sign-Up page. I usually uncheck all of them except phone. If they provide their phone number, that's cool. Eventually, we will probably try a short SMS or text messaging service. We have not started that yet, but I like to gather that information anyway.

If you want to do a quiz when people sign up for your webinar, GoToWebinar lets you do that.

"After registering, registrants will receive an email with information on joining the Webinar." Answer Yes to this one.

Then you may redirect registrants to a particular web page. When we talk about the money-getting section, here you can send them to some sort of continuity offer.

Next, click Save and "Email me the invitation."

Now, you are going to get an email with links to go to the webinar registration signup form.

It's as simple as that. Now, all you have to do is wait until your date. You sign in 10 to 15 minutes early. You click Start and then you will be rocking and rolling from there. It really is just an awesome service.

For automated webinars, we use EverWebinar.com. It has become the premiere service for this. It comes with some pretty impressive bonuses and a 30-day guarantee. It has a very flexible advanced scheduling system. It can do Just-in-Time webinars that start a few minutes after someone registers, or you can have it start the webinar at a specific time if you prefer.

EverWebinar has a pretty robust email system built-in, so in many cases we put our post-webinar followup email sequences right in EverWebinar rather than our autoresponder service. It also handle pre-webinar emails if you want it to. EverWebinar also integrates with just about all software that you can imagine. It has lots of analytics and reports so you can see in-depth exactly how your webinars are performing.

Another interesting feature of EverWebinar is called Hybrid Webinars. This lets you chat live with your attendees while your prerecorded webinar plays. Of course, that means you have to be there to do this, but it lets you focus on interacting and frees you from having to do the presentation again and again. A good way to use this is to monitor which days and times get the most attendees to your replays, then just show up to chat for those times. For example, if it turns out that your Tuesday and Thursday night replays draw the biggest crowds, you could be on those to run the chats those nights and just let your replays run on autopilot the rest of the week.

We've also used StealthSeminar.com for automated webinars. You are going to have to go through some of the documentation in order to set it up correctly, and, while you may not need a tech guy, you might want somebody who is more tech-savvy to set it up. It's reliable, it doesn't go down, and you get excellent customer service. They will even set up your webinar for you. If you have any issues whatsoever, you email Support and they will get back to you within an average of 7 minutes. It's ridiculous.

StealthSeminar.com is a bulletproof service. It integrates with all kinds of services and is also available on every platform that you could want.

Once you actually join StealthSeminar.com, they have a pretty extensive on-boarding process, which is going to give you enough information to get started.

The thing about automated webinars is that there isn't an industry standard. Everybody is trying to create their own automated webinar platform and be that industry standard. It's just something to be aware of.

In some of the Facebook groups I am in, and in some of the Skype conversations that I've had, everybody is still looking for the one that solves all their problems, but there isn't one yet. This is unfortunate, because there are so many pieces of the puzzle that are out there, but it's just not 100% there yet.

Once you decide which system is right for you, all of them have really great support and tutorials on how to get set up. It is a technical operation to set up a webinar. What I recommend to my personal clients is to do a few live webinars. Pick the best one, the one that converts the best, the one that has the best response and feedback, and then set it up on one of the automated webinar platforms, StealthSeminars.com still being our recommended choice. See if it works nearly as well as being live. Automated hardly ever out-converts live, but it is worth a shot, and something you should try. Just use the replay of the real webinar that you did.

Don't sit in your office and do a video and then automate it. You're not going to get the right *liveness,* or the right energy, or answer the questions the way that you should, even if you have any questions to answer. So, I always recommend doing a live webinar, doing it for even just 10 or 15 people, and then automating it after that. See if it works. If it does, fantastic. If it converts nearly as well, then that's awesome. If it doesn't, then do a couple more live webinars. With the automated webinar, you'll just want to test and try a few different things and move on from there.

Getting People Signed Up

In this chapter, we're going to talk about webinar registration (AKA signup) pages. Signup pages themselves come down to a couple of very key elements and the reason why webinars work so well. In order to actually attend the webinar, somebody has to sign up for it. It's like an opt-in form and that's one of the beauties of webinars and why they're so prevalent.

Not very many marketers or affiliates will send traffic to an opt-in form because that basically delays payment. They would rather send people right to a sales letter. Webinars are the exception. They will happily mail you the signup form for a webinar because they know that, in order for somebody to purchase, they have to be on the webinar.

That's one of the reasons webinars are such incredible list-building tools, not to mention when people see a webinar signup page, they are more likely to sign up, because they're going to be given something live and free, and they then can make the choice to purchase.

This is also a big reason why I advise you to do a webinar instead if you're ever tempted to do a very long video sales letter (30 minutes or longer). I'll cover video sales letters in a later chapter.

So, webinar signup pages are basically treated just like normal opt-in pages. When you break an opt-in page down, there are basically four elements to it. There is the title; there is the body copy; there are the bullets—the features and benefits—and, then there's a call to action. The call to action is for somebody to sign up for the webinar itself. The only difference is that you really have to sell the benefits of being on the webinar, so they actually show up.

That's one of the biggest hurdles of webinars now: people will sign up and then not show up. That's an issue because in order for somebody to purchase, they need to actually see what it is you're selling. So you need to do everything possible to get them to attend the webinar, not just sign up for it.

The first thing is the headline. This is where your topic really comes back up. We talked in an earlier section about topics and here is where it really plays out. You can create a headline from a topic and it is going to frame the entire webinar, and exactly what you are teaching.

Here are some examples:

- **5 Foods You Should Avoid When Losing Weight**—that's a great webinar title and it's also a great headline. The headline and the webinar title oftentimes go hand-in-hand.

- **How to Make $100 a Day**—another one that we have used very successfully in the past and that kind of keys in succinctly to what people's burning desire is. Their burning desire is not necessarily to make $10,000 a day. Most people know intrinsically that they can't do that, but they can make $100 a day, and if they make $100 a day, then they will be able to quit their day job or pay some of the bills, or whatever else it is. It is a great middle ground, a great sticking point to use in a headline.

- **3 Gardening Techniques That You Should Be Using**—again, there is a certain curiosity play here. Anyone interested in gardening is going to want to know what those three techniques are, and you can further quantify that by adding a feature or benefit into this headline. 3 Gardening Techniques That Will Help You Grow a Beautiful Garden or 3 Gardening Techniques That Will Make Sure That Your Vegetables Won't Get Washed Out.

- **7 Ways to Increase Your Productivity in an Hour or Less**—people look at that and think "I would love to get more work done in less time, and if you tell me that that there's seven ways I can increase productivity in under an hour, then that's fantastic!"

The headline is really that initial grab. It is the initial interaction between you and the prospect that is going to make them want to sign up for your webinar. A good headline is going to solidify what you want folks to sign up for. It's going to lay out exactly what you're going to go over in the webinar, exactly what they're going to learn, and the features and benefits that are going to be delivered by them attending the webinar.

It's also going to give your webinar structure, much like a mission statement. I sometimes get a bit deep into business theory and process, and one of the things that gets into is mission statements. A good mission statement will help you focus what it is you do from a business standpoint, and what you do day-to-day to actually bring revenue through the door. A good webinar headline is very much the same thing. First of all, it is a good headline; second of all, it's a good webinar title; and, third of all, it's a good framework that you can use to actually deliver the webinar.

After you think of that headline, and think of the webinar title itself, everything else just falls into place, because the structure of the webinar is really very simple. There is an introduction, and then there is the content, and the content is going to play right into what this headline should be.

So, for instance, "7 Ways to Increase Your Productivity in an Hour or Less": first of all, in an hour or less is great, because the webinar is going to be under an hour; and if we deliver seven productivity tips that are going to be helpful for people who attend, then all we really have to do is just devote a slide or two to each of the seven productivity tips, and talk through them, provide a couple of examples, get a little bit of prospect feedback, and then you end with a pitch.

The body copy is the second element of the signup page, and this is where you can substantiate the headline. First of all, you want to try to be personal, so "Join us for a webinar." People like to buy from people, not businesses. When you're personal, when you're inviting, when you're not just a corporate figurehead, when you're not a logo, this helps frame you as an expert. It helps people bond to you, and that's one of the beauties of webinars, that they help bond prospects to you in a way that most marketing does not.

Even if you asked for a sale at the end of the call, people hang out with you for 45 minutes, 50 minutes, an hour, before you start pitching. There's a lot of rapport-building that happens in that hour, and, especially if you follow the framework we talk about here in this book, you're going to deliver a lot of value, and people are really going to love you for it.

At the end, yes, there is a pitch. Yes, you can invite people to purchase something from you which is going to aid their training or aid their development a bit further, but as long as you are personal through the interaction, and on the signup page, then people are going to continue to see you as being the expert.

You want to convey that it is a training session. A lot of people know that if they are going to a webinar, they are going to be pitched, so you want to really play up the training aspect. You're going to get 45 minutes of training in these seven productivity tools, these five gardening tips, these three foods... You are really going to want to play up the information that you're going to be giving them before the pitch and actually key in with what some of the features and benefits are.

The body copy does not need to be any longer than 100 words or so. You want to make sure that there are obvious benefits in your body copy. If an affiliate is promoting it, if somebody else is actually mailing their list for your webinar, include their name on the signup page.

One of the things I like to do is, "Joe Affiliate Presents 5 Foods You Shouldn't Eat" or "Randy Affiliate Presents 7 Productivity Tools That You Need in Your Business." Don't have any more than 100 to 200 words for the body. You don't need any more than that. The rest is going to be filled out in the features and benefits section.

For the features and benefits on the signup page, this is really a fun little experience, not only in these signup pages, but in copywriting in general. As with any copy, features and benefits should be well outlined. So, a feature is a descriptive element and a benefit is why it matters.

For example, in your webinar signup page, "We'll reveal the number-one food item in your shopping cart that is preventing your weight loss, so that when you cut it out, you can feel the excess fall right off, and drop a dress size the same week."

So, the feature will reveal the number one food item in your shopping cart that is preventing your weight loss. The benefit, why it matters, is so that when you cut it out, you can feel the excess fall right off, and you drop a dress size in one week. That's the benefit. That's why it matters.

One of the things about features and benefits is that people don't buy features. People buy benefits. You don't buy a drill, you buy the hole it's going to make. It's the same way to think about the features and benefits in your signup page or your sales copy or your opt-in pages. Always provide the feature and the benefit together.

Another example is: "You will discover the top time-killer in your day and what to do to avoid it, so you can turn your 8-hour workday into a turbocharged day that delivers 20 hours worth of work." So, the feature is the top time-killer in your day and what to do to avoid it; the benefit is that you can turn your 8-hour workday into a new turbocharged day.

SO is BIG here. You can see in these 2 examples that *SO* is right in the middle. *SO* is like that the glue between the feature and the benefit. Don't ever leave something hanging without a *SO*. Always make sure that there is *SO* in the page, or some sort of a binding element between the feature and the benefit.

Lastly, the call to action is what is at the bottom of the signup page. The call to action is the most important part of this whole page, because without a call to action, people just visit the page and leave. You need to tell them what to do next.

For example, "Sign up below before seats fill up." Or "Enter your name and email below, so your seat is saved."

Try to blend in scarcity, because attendee lines are limited on webinars, so depending on the package by your webinar service, you may have 100 or 500 or 1,000 or whatever the limit it. Try to blend in scarcity.

Also, we've had some luck with prizes, not in getting signups, but in getting them to show up for the webinar. So, give away a free Kindle or iPad. Give them a little bit of a bonus, a little bit of a guilty incentive, to actually show up. If they attend the whole webinar, and actually listen to what it is you have to say, you're going to give away an iPad to an attendee.

Offer the product in exchange for the prize. So, at the end of the webinar, you look at your attendees list and you say, "Okay, Big Joe, you just won a Kindle! How about double or nothing? How about what we do is, I will give you the course for free in exchange for the Kindle?" Oftentimes, actually most of the time, they say yes.

Now, if they don't say yes, they want the Kindle, then obviously, you have to send them the Kindle. Oftentimes, they will trade that prize they just won for the course, because they get the course for free—and it doesn't cost you anything to deliver the course.

A twist on this is to give some freebie to every attendee who is on the webinar at that point in time. This should be the same type of freebie you would use to build a list, or maybe something a bit more valuable. The main point is that people have to attend the webinar and stay on until you give that item out, and you don't email them the link, you just show them the link during the webinar.

If you follow these guidelines, your webinar signup page is going to convert in the high 30 to 40% range. You might be able to get 50 to 55% depending on the topic. In some niches, webinars are going to convert a little higher than others, because people haven't seen them as often. Make sure to test different signup pages as you go, too. If 1,000 people see a page, a 1% difference means 10 more people.

Say you have a couple of webinars in a row, have the first webinar be your constant, your control, and then on the next webinar, test a little bit of a different headline. If you can bump your conversion percentage by 1%, that means 10 more people that are thinking about buying.

Later in this book we're going to go through different numbers, EPCs, EPAs, and that's all money. That's cash in the bank stuff. Just having a 1% conversion increase on your signup page can be the difference of $5,000 or $10,000 in sales, once it all washes out at the end.

Your signup page really is the beginning of where you can start testing and making differences, making the changes and tweaks that make you a lot of money.

Webinar Reminders

Webinar reminders are really important, and the reason I'm saying this is because most of the automated webinar platforms don't have a good reminder system.

GoToWebinar is the industry standard and they have a good reminders system. They send out a reminder one day before and then about an hour or two hours before to the webinar. MeetingBurner and EverWebinar are also pretty good in this regard, then you're going to want to make sure that you set up reminders in your email autoresponder service, in your email platform.

Overall, reminders are pretty simple. So, "Hey, the '5 Secret Foods' webinar is starting in an hour. Here's your link…" You want to make sure that they get sent out.

The thing about human nature is that you don't sign up for a webinar, and then go over and pencil it into your calendar, and set up reminders for yourself. Generally, you add your email to the signup box and you save it in your inbox and then you forget about it. Without a reminder of any kind, then your actual show-up rates are going to be pretty dismal.

Some automated systems do it well by default. StealthSeminars has a feature that is okay. EverWebinar is pretty good. GoToWebinars does it by default—you can even set up weekly webinars where your listeners only have to sign up once, and then they send reminders out for every single webinar that you have.

The Presentation

In this chapter, I will walk through what your presentation should flow like and what it should look like. This is the most important part of the entire webinar training in this book. Your presentations are going to make or break your success, because it's all about the training!

Here's the anatomy of the presentation:

- **Slide 1:** The name of your presentation. So, "5 Foods You Should Be Eating." It's the first thing people see. When they sign in, five or ten minutes before the webinar, this slide should be what they're looking at.

- **Slide 2:** This is what people are going to learn by the end of the call. These are your features and benefits. You can copy and paste them from your signup page. You want to make sure that people know what to expect during the call and what they're going to be learning during the webinar, even before you start.

  There is a great saying, "In order to have an effective stage presence, an effective presentation, you teach them what they are going to learn, then you teach them, and then you teach them what you just taught them." You intro them, you give them the content, and then you close by saying this is what we went through. It works tremendously well. You can see it in education all across the board.

- **Slide 3:** Who you are. A picture, a short biography, why it matters. For the most part, people who come to your webinar do not know who you are. They have no idea, nor do they really care. They're there for information; they are there to be taught; they are there to see if you are actually a subject matter expert, and if they should follow you and listen to you and actually care.

So, in Slide 3, you intro yourself: a little picture, a little about me, and talk a little bit about why it matters, what you've been through, what some of your awards are, maybe if you graduated college and what your degree is, and what you been doing for the last few years. Any more than one or two slides, and people will think, *This guy is full of himself.* I, personally, like to keep this at one slide.

- **Slides 4 through 7:** The Big Problem. Sum up the overall problem that you're trying to solve. This needs to be well-crafted. You want to drive some pain points home, and really anchor the audience to the reason why they are there in the first place. So, with the "5 Foods You Should be Eating," the audience is probably struggling with weight loss. They may have issues with their diet, they've been working out for the past few years, or they have tried severa; different fad diets, and nothing has worked.

  Really drive some of these pain points home. Talk to the audience and even ask them questions. "How long have you been trying to lose weight? Have you had any success?" Just talk. The beauty of live webinars is that they can be give-and-take. You can get a feel for what the audience is doing through the comment box.

- **Slides 8 through 20:** You deliver the content. This is where you get into the meat of the webinar. "The 5 Things….." or "The 7 Tools…" or "The 3 Gardening Tips…" or whatever. Whatever you told them they would be learning, this is where you deliver it on these 12 slides. Sometimes, in this section of the webinar, we go longer. It's OK if this part ends up being 20-40 slides; there is nothing magic about the number 12.

- **Slide 21:** The Bridge. This where you go from the content and the training to the pitch. Here are some ways to start, to kick that off: "We have covered a lot of stuff in this presentation…" or "Obviously, I couldn't pack everything into this hour-long call…" or "So, I created this training product, and it is called Fat Loss Tips…"

This bridge takes you from training into pitch, or into sale. For example, "We covered a lot of stuff in this presentation, and I'm sure your head's just swimming. There were some great tips, some great tutorials, foods, etc., but this is just the tip of the iceberg. In fact, what we did is put together a training program, because we're getting so many amazing questions through these webinars. We put it all together in a video course, and it's called _____."

- **Slide 22:** Go through the product. Describe the features and benefits of the product, show product shots like box images or e-book images, using Slides 23 through 26. Don't drag this out too long, because they've been through training, to a bridge, to now looking at your product, and they are thinking, *Do I want this? Should I buy this?*

- **Slide 27:** Call to action. "This whole system is only $37. Just go to XYZ.com/webinar to sign-up for it." That's your pitch. You just pitched them on your product. So, I've seen it happen where presenters hit that bridge, and they are doing fine, and then they go into the product. However, the product is just so big that they try to put 25 slides into talking about the product. The product portion is way, way longer than the content portion that was just delivered. That's an issue because people's attention is going to wane, and they are going to sign off. If they get too bored with this product, then they are going to leave. The call to action is going to be a dollar figure or just a URL.

- **Slides 28-31:** Testimonials. Immediately after the call to action, if you have some testimonials, you can add them here. You can have 3-4 slides with "people who bought our system, or bought our product, or bought our program, and this is what they've been able to experience because of their purchase."

- **Slide 32:** Guarantee. You always want to tell them about a guarantee on a webinar, so a 30-day guarantee, a 60-day guarantee, a one-year guarantee, a *Scout's Honor* guarantee, whatever you want to do. I usually include the link to the Support Desk right here, too. It's a nice goodwill gesture.

- **Slide 33:** Bonuses. If you're including any fast action bonuses, this is where they would be.

- **Slide 34:** Questions. "Any questions you have? Go ahead, fire away. I'm going to be here to answer questions for the next 30 or 45 minutes. I want to make sure that whatever rebuttals, whatever feedback you may have about the training, we'll get it answered." This is a slide you are going to hang out on. I have seen questions last for 2 hours; it is totally up to you how long you want to do questions.

Just be aware that most of the people buy while you are answering questions. They don't buy because you very simply showed them the Call to Action. The question time is where you exhibit your expertise. When one person asks a question, you better believe 10 or 20 people have the same question, but just haven't asked it.

The question and answer period is a great way to exhibit your knowledge, and is also going to be where you get most of your sales. If no one is asking questions, then grab some questions from past webinars. Keep in mind that on Slide 27 to 34, make sure that that URL is on the bottom on every page, so that people always have immediate access to it.

Make that URL short and sweet so it's easy for people to type in. Also put the URL in the chat box, because in some webinar systems, that will make it a live link. Obviously, people can't click on a link on your slide. (OK, they can click, but it won't take them to your site!)

Your Performance

In this chapter, we will discuss your performance on the webinar. This is the nitty-gritty. Everything that was done up until this point was just setting up the webinar. This is where you actually get on and start going through the webinar: you have a live audience, you have question and answer, and one of the things I really want to get across today is the need for confidence, the need for poise, and just getting up, getting out there, and getting started.

When I first started doing webinars, it was daunting to me to even have 10 people on a webinar just listening to me talk. What if I screw up? What if my Internet goes down? What if all of these unknown things happened? How do you deal with that stuff?

Quite honestly, when I first started a few years ago, I was quite an introvert. I didn't like talking; I didn't like talking in public; I didn't like the fact that people could hear my voice on the other end of the webinar. It was rough. This section is going to help you squelch that.

It turns out this is very common. Even some people who speak on stage at big events get nervous about doing webinars. So if you're nervous about doing them, don't worry.

We'll be doing a lot of talking about every element of the performance itself, from the proper structure of a webinar, to how you should perform verbally, along with giving you permission to do certain things. I'm also going to talk about some money-getting strategies, some things that we have seen work, and that have worked for us. We are also going to get into the question and answer section, and why it is the most important part.

We are going to talk about some webinar etiquette. I want to prepare you a little bit for some the things that are going to happen on a webinar, so that you know in advance of going into one. I will also give you some top tips that always seem work really well. The top tips section is probably the best of this section of the book. We've run hundreds of webinars with lots of different styles and lots of different sequences, and with different elements thrown into them, so the tips section is going to be huge for you.

The Structure

Here we will discuss the structure of your webinar and what you need to do to actually pull off successful, high-converting webinars.

There are two general styles of webinars that you're going to be doing. There's one with a co-host, where you are talking with somebody else—and this sometimes makes it easier—or you are going to be doing it on your own. When you are on your own, you are the only one who is performing, and it really is a performance. Some people do it better than others. Some people are more dry; some people are more animated and action-oriented, but no matter how you look at it, it is a performance.

When I say it's a performance, I don't mean it's fake or that you will be reading a script, just that you will be putting on a presentation for the public, and that means there are certain considerations you should keep in mind.

If you're doing it with somebody else, it's going to have a different dynamic than if you are doing it on your own. If you're just getting started, unless you have a partner, or somebody who is helping you with your business, you're probably going to be doing it alone. I started doing it alone. I had no connections, no friends in this space, so I didn't have anybody else to go to to bounce ideas off of, or questions. It was just me, going through it, providing some training, and then closing it up.

=As people start to promote your webinar, you start to get more opportunities to work with a co-host. One of the biggest things in the affiliate marketing game is, if somebody emails to your webinar, and you generate 500, 700 or 1,000 attendees on your webinar, then first of all, those attendees are yours, and, second of all, that person whose list that is is probably going to jump on the webinar with you, and actually be your co-host. They are going to introduce you. They are going to be there to bounce questions off of, or be there to ask for some more clarification on some of the content of the training. But do not let that be a barrier of entry to you; don't let you not having a cohost bother you up front. The first couple webinars are going to be on your own.

If you're running solo on the webinar, here some things to keep in mind. First, you introduce yourself. "Hey, this is Jason. Thanks so much for joining us on this webinar. We're going to walk you through 5 very simple tips that you can use today to start losing weight."

Just to make sure that that all the tech stuff is dialed in, always ask the question, "Can everybody hear me okay?" Tell them what to do: answer in the comment box or the chat box. Just make sure they can hear you and they can see your screen. Tell them, "One of the issues with live presentations is that sometimes technology gets the better of us. It is just a fact of the matter, but the point is, this is live, and I'm really excited to be able to answer some questions for you, and deliver some training, to get rock and rolling." So, it's a very comfortable and easy way to get everything started.

Asking your audience to type the answer to a simple question also gets them engaged and paying closer attention to you. It gets them to follow a minor call to action, what some people call a micro commitment, that makes them more likely to respond when you give them the call to action to buy your offer.

Some people like to do a little bit of a pre-game. Two of my best friends, Ryan Moran and Travis Sago, do this very well. They are on and bantering, talking back and forth about some tips or tricks, or what they've seen working, and it is just kind of a nice segue into the first few minutes of the webinar. Say you have a 9 a.m. webinar: people are going to be logging in at 8:45 or 8:50, all the way up to 9:05 and later, so the idea is to kind of have a little bit of a dialogue or banter with the audience for the first couple of minutes of the scheduled webinar. It gives people a chance to jump into the call.

Start the presentation about 4 minutes after the scheduled start. You'll start going through the presentation slide-by-slide, so once you get past the second and third slide, everything unfolds as it should. The PowerPoint slides are going to cue your presentation, and everything is now scripted.

The hardest part is the intro. That used to be the part that scared me the most: *How am I going to introduce myself? What am I going to say?* The point that you should keep in the back of your mind is that they are there because you're going to give them training, information, ideas, etc. You are the star, and you need think of it that way. You don't need to be cocky or conceited about it, but you need to understand that they signed in to listen to you. It is your obligation to give them value, to give them what they want, and also to entertain them a little bit, to be the professional. It's always good to start off with a little dialogue.

It is also a good idea to bring someone on who just answers all the questions in the question box. If you're just running solo, that is totally fine, but if you have an employee or partner or whatever, and maybe they don't want to be your co-host and have their voice on the webinars, then just ask them to answer questions.

Some of the most successful webinars I have ever seen have a few different people on the call. There's the host, and there's the cohost, the two people interacting back and forth, and then they have a least one person whose sole job is to answer questions in that text box. They are typing answers as people are asking questions. The nice thing about it is that the host and the co-host don't have to worry about the questions until the end, yet as people come up with timely questions, they can get immediate answers. Once you get to the end, and you open up for Q&A time, you can go through the answers and then you close it down.

With a co-host, if you have somebody else on the line with you, he or she is probably going to introduce you. They'll talk a little bit about how they met you, what their experience has been with you, their friendship with you, and then they will introduce you. Again, you will have some minor chit-chat for a few minutes before kicking it off, to allow for the remaining folks to jump on the line.

Once you get introduced, say, "Okay, can everyone hear me okay? Is the sound good? Where is everybody from?" Read off where everybody is from: the U.K., Chicago, San Diego, Pakistan, etc. This is *social proof*, meaning that attendees listening see that there are people joining in from all around the world. There was one webinar, back when I first got started, and what they did was actually open up all the lines. They had a few hundred people on the call, and they opened up all the lines, so all you heard was talking, babies crying, and everything else all fighting within the line. Then they closed it off and said that's what happens when you have thousands of people on one webinar! That's why mics are not enabled on everybody's connection.

There is a certain element of social proof, when you're reading where people are from, when you open up the lines like that, and it really just helps attendees see that, yes, you are the star; yes, they should be on this call, because you're going to be giving away some great information.

After the introduction, your co-host is probably going to mute themselves, and then you take over, rocking and rolling with the content.

As you go through the presentation slide-by-slide, your co-host may jump back in, asking questions, or clarifying something for the audience.

One of the things that I personally like to do is, every 3 or 4 slides, I'll go look at the questions to see if there's anything that's pertinent to exactly what I'm talking about, and then continue with the presentation. I don't stop the middle for a plethora of questions, but once in a while, there will be something that I'll toss in really quick. That's totally your call. You can either answer them in the middle of your show, or you can wait till the end—it's totally up to you.

As I mentioned previously, it helps to bring somebody that just answers questions in the question box, but it's more of an advanced tip. When you're just getting started, you don't necessarily need to worry about that.

You'll get all the way to the call to action, and your co-host will jump back in, generally. This is the normal etiquette of a co-host-style webinar. So, you go through the pitch: "Go to domainname.com/webinar to get started…" and talk a little bit about your guarantee, and then normally, your cohost is going to jump back in and tell the audience, because they are his or her people, why they need to buy the products, or why they recommend buying your product.

Then it ends with normal Q&A time. There are going to be questions back and forth between you, the co-host and the audience. The co-host may have some questions of his own for you, and those questions are generally designed to talk to the greatest number of people.

Sometimes this Q&A session lasts up to an hour and a half after the webinar, which is a little long, honestly. The webinar in its entirety should only last about an hour and a half. We are going to talk a little bit more about Q&A later on this module, because the Q&A section itself is where you're going to get the most sales.

When you are working with someone else, sometimes there's some lag in the microphone, so just bear with it. Every once in a while, depending on the Internet connection between you and your co-host, there is little bit of a lag, so you want to try to avoid jumping over each other's voices very much. Some of it is going to happen, so just keep that in mind.

Some people want to talk more than others. Sometimes, if you're working with a co-host, they will want to jump in, to have their voice heard very, very often, and other times they just want to mute themselves. Other times, they may not even be on, and they will tell you, "I will come in, I will introduce you, and then I will sign off," and then you just take over from there.

One of the biggest things you can do on the webinar is announce buyers. After the call to action, and during the Q&A session, say, "For those of you that are buying, let me give you a shout-out. Post in the question box that you purchased, and I'll call your name out." People love it. People love social proof; they also love hearing their name knowing that 500 people are also on this call. You can say, "Hey, thanks so much, Don, for purchasing. We're so happy to have you."

When audience members hear other people's names being called after buying the product, they feel they aren't the only ones out there wanting to buy the product. The social aspect of the call is huge with getting people to buy. Announcing buyers is fantastic. The biggest webinars that I have ever had have done this and announced buyers.

For introverts, or those not very confident with technology, you can screw up. Tell them "This is live, so anything goes." Use it as a benefit. "This isn't automated in any way. It's live and I'm sitting here with my four dogs on the other end of the line here, looking at my computer, and I am so happy to have you here." I've had my internet die with 600 people on the line. I'm not saying that that was a fantastic thing, but it went out for five or seven minutes. Out of 600 people, maybe 30 or 40 people logged out, because they thought it was over, but the majority of them stayed on. I just picked up and we still had a really great webinar. We still sold $10,000 or $15,000 worth of product.

I always have misspellings in my PowerPoint. I don't necessarily edit things quite as well as I probably should. Sometimes I include the wrong link in the slide or the wrong affiliate. If Joe is my co-host and the one promoting my webinar, I'll have last week's link for Bob. In the slide, it will be domainname.com/Bob, and then I'll have to exit out of the webinar, or exit out of the PowerPoint, change the link, put it back up there, and say to everybody who wants to buy this product, it is domainname.com/Joe.

Sometimes the audio doesn't come through as clear as you like. It's totally okay what happens, because you are doing live. It's an event and it's not scripted, so it's anything goes.

You will make sales as long as you offer something for sale. That's all there is to it. If you offer something, you will sell something.

The Call To Action

In this chapter, we're going to be talking about the call to action (or CTA) to use on a webinar. Put simply, the "money-getting." I did my best and went back through a few years of notes and data to pull these out.

The goal of a webinar is to make money, point blank.

With webinars, you don't need to have perfect sales copy, or even sales copy at all. It comes down to three very simple pieces:

- The introduction
- The story
- The pitch

You don't need to pay somebody $15,000 to write a sales letter. You don't need to do any of that stuff. You need have a webinar and a way for them to purchase your product.

There are some specific money-getting strategies and principles that we have tested, and that's what this this chapter is about. You can mix these in, but you don't have to. If you have a few webinars under your belt, awesome, this should super-charge them. If not, combine these strategies into them when you feel comfortable. Some of these things are a little advanced, and you may not feel comfortable, and if it's your first webinar, then some of them might be a little bit of a pain.

The first thing that I absolutely love doing is the *fast action bonus*. "If you buy within the next 15 minutes, you get this." In the most successful webinars that I've ever done, we do fast action bonuses. It can be a digital product or a physical product. I like physical.

The first time I did this was with a physical DVD mailing. It was a product that I was really jazzed about. In the webinar, I included one very simple slide. It was titled fast action bonus: "If you buy within the next 15 minutes, I'm going to send you these two DVDs." I Googled and found this online stopwatch and put it up on screen, so all the attendees could see it.

I put 15 minutes on it, hit Start, and started answering all the Q&A stuff. I just told them you have 15 minutes to buy this. People started buying and then I started doing some call-outs. "Oh, thanks, John. Thanks, Joe. Thanks, Sally." All of a sudden, everybody started buying. So, 7 minutes, 6 minutes, 5 minutes, 4 minutes, all the way down and at the two-minute mark, I said "For everybody who is the Shopping Cart and ordering the product, just let me know here, so I know to make sure to send you the bonuses."

Then everybody started rocking and rolling. Then I said, "You only have a minute left. If you have any problems with the checkout process, or if you're in the middle of checkout, then make sure we know, so we can get you your bonus." I had that announcement at two minutes and at one minute. The product was $97 and the conversion rate 52%, which means if 100 were on the call, 52 people bought. Typically, for a $97 product, the conversion rates can be about 25 to 30%.

We doubled our conversion rate by offering this fast action bonus. At the end, there were a couple of people that said, "I really, really want your product. I don't have my credit card," or "I want to talk to my wife about this first. Can you give me an extension?" I told them, "I totally understand that you want to check with your wife," or "If you don't have a way to pay for it, that's not your fault. So, what I'll do is I will give you 24-hour extension." They so appreciated the extension that we ended up getting sales for the next several days.

It worked like gangbusters. Fast action bonuses are my number one tip. I didn't even have any physical DVDs at that point—I didn't even know what was I going to put on the DVDs. I just named the DVDs and said people would get them for free. The next day, I had to go purchase myself a DVD-maker, because I ended up selling so much on the first webinar that I now had to make over 175 DVDs.

Also, do attendee bonuses. They are really pretty simple. Offer an iPad or a Kindle as a bonus. "So, if you attend the webinar, and you stay on until the end of the webinar, then I'm going to randomly choose one person in the list, and give you an iPad or Kindle." This is all the way into the question and answer section, and after the pitch. So, you give somebody an incentive to stay on all the way through the pitch, and then perhaps they may win.

Once you announce the winner, follow up with "I'll tell you what—if you want, I'll trade you Product X. I'll give you our product at a $997 value for the iPad that you just won." Call it your Double-or-Nothing Guarantee. They almost always take product access. Almost always. Every once in a while, you'll see someone take the iPad or the Kindle, but generally they'll take the product.

I have also done this with free downloads like process maps. I say, "I will offer a free MindMap on the process that we use in our business for exactly what we're talking about today, but the reason we're giving it away at the end is because you actually have to have some understanding about what we're doing, so you need to stay on through the call, and I'll give the MindMap at the end. Everything is going to come together and make a lot more sense." When we did it, we gave it to everyone on the call.

Another really successful money-getting strategy is one that I have only ever seen one person do. We tested it and it worked like crazy. It was: Don't talk about price on the webinar at all. Don't say anything about price. Say, "Go to domain.com/sign-up" as a Call to Action. No prices, nothing.

If they're interested in the product, they are then going to type the URL into their browser. That way, you don't have to worry about pricing or money. Some people do strange things when asking for money. If it's in my case, I don't like asking for money. I just don't. This allows you to bypass the whole thing, but still have effective webinars. They can go and discover how much you're going to be asking for your product.

I learned this from a guy who does this successfully—his product is $997. In his first webinar, he was really very uncomfortable about saying this product was $997. He just included the domain with the $997 price and it worked so well that he continued the practice.

The thing I like the most about this method is: first, you don't have to talk about money; and second, you can split test various prices. What is the product worth? What is this webinar or the sales message worth? What do people expect to pay with a webinar that you just delivered? I suggested this to my friend, and he had not heard of this. I asked him if he had ever done a split test with his product. His product was $997. Had he ever tested $497 or $997 or $1,997?

I went on to tell him that he was sending his customers to a domain, so why not create 3 sales pages and see which price outperforms the others? It is very simple to do. All you have to do is create 3 variations of that sales page, one with $497, one with $997, and one with $1,997.

You'll need a piece of software: for example, Google has Website Optimizer. It's free. The one that we like to use is Visual Website Optimizer. All it does is when somebody goes to this domain, split up what they see into these 3 versions. It will send the first person to $497, the second one to $997, and the third one to $1,997. It will round-robin them and send an equal number of people to the split tests.

Say you have four people buy at $497, and two people buy at $1,997, you've just doubled your money. You make $2,000 more by offering the same product. It's really pretty simple and it's wildly effective.

This works really well if you don't say a price on the webinar. People are going to be attending the webinar from all over the world. They have no idea what price somebody else is seeing. It's not unethical. People do it all the time. Big Fortune 500 companies test prices before they actually send something to the market. This way you can you can figure out how much people are willing to spend for your product.

You can also save face if your product is high dollar. You don't have to ask for money. Introverts are going to understand this. One of the reasons I don't sell $2,000 products is because it's difficult for me to ask for $2,000. Plus, when you go to automate your webinar, you don't have to change pricing, which could involve expensive video editing. You don't have to worry about anything because the domain names can be the same across the board and it will be a split test from there.

Another money-getting strategy that we really like is when the signup page is an offer. Someone goes to sign up for the event, and the page that they are directed to immediately afterwards—there is a setting in all webinar platforms that says where should users be directed to—says, "Thanks so much for signing up. While I have you here, I would really like to tell you about this new program that we have…"

This is a fantastic money-making opportunity that most people ignore. Send them to some product that you're selling, so that you can start to monetize those leads. People are uniquely tuned into your message when they sign up for your webinar, so if a thank you page says, "Thanks for signing up! While I have you here, check this out…" then people are going to react to it. Normally, those pages get 6 to 10% sign-ups, but some of those people won't be attending the webinar, so it's money you wouldn't have had otherwise.

Another thing that I really like to do is a post-webinar survey. Although not tied directly to money, surveys after the webinar are awesome for collecting testimonials and the good things people have to say, which you can use in your future marketing materials. Some of the best testimonials I have ever received have been done this way. You can put them on your site, in your sales copy, or wherever you want.

After the webinar finishes, a window pops up, and there will be a form in there. You just very simply ask them what they liked, what they didn't like, and what they want more of. Be sure to tell them that some of their answers may be used for testimonials. You do have to actually tell them what you're going to be using the answers for, but it's a fantastic way to get good testimonials.

Q&A Session

In this chapter, we are going to talk about Q&A. The Q&A session is probably the most important part of the entire webinar because this is where most of the sales are going to come from. Q&A stands for question and answer. Q&A happens throughout the presentation, and also at the end.

As you're going through your webinar, as you are teaching, and training, and delivering content and value, viewers are reacting to what you are talking about. Oftentimes, they react in the form of asking questions during presentation. They also will react when you ask them questions looking for feedback, which is awesome. You always want to encourage people to type into the question box, get answers, and help dictate the way your presentation goes.

I do this in a couple of different ways. First off, you want to start off early. If you remember in the introduction, we said that you start off by asking, "Can everybody hear me? Can everybody see my screen?" When you ask that, you're starting to train them to use the question box. The next question is, "Where is everybody from?" And they start to reply with wherever they are from. So, they are being trained to answer in the question box.

Then what I really enjoy doing is asking questions. With selling on a webinar, you want to hit somebody's pain point. You want to figure out why it is they were drawn to your webinar and what they're hoping to achieve by viewing the webinar, and also, what they hope to achieve by buying your product. The question box can be your best friend in that scenario.

So, for example, as you start your pitch, as you work with a pain point and try to figure out what people's emotions are based around that pain point, you can ask them: "How much money would you like to make per day? What would make a difference in your life? What would you do with that money?" Get them interactive.

One of the things that I did in my "Money-Saving Secrets" webinar was we would go through and pick a niche, and in that niche, I would go in and figure out all the different ways that I would make money in that niche, just point blank, right on the webinar. I would always ask attendees, "What niche are you in? What would you like to go through?" Then I would pick one of those, because this helps them figure out and learn the process of doing what we do. It also gets them interactive and motivated to buy your product and consume your training.

Also, you can post something controversial and get people's reactions. So, you can talk about something that might be a little bit off-the-cuff. But, a word of warning: people can get pretty irate and belligerent, because they may feel that you're the only one that actually sees the questions, or your co-host. The first few webinars I did, once in a while, I would get a reaction that really rubbed me the wrong way.

So, during your presentation, it is encouraged to gauge feedback live. Ask questions and provide some "live" stuff. For example, "Help me pick a niche." "What do you think the first food is?" "What is the number one food that grocery stores sell out of in times of crisis?" Actually do a little poll, a little challenge.

I usually answer a few questions after every few slides, and I'll tell the audience that at the beginning. I will say, "Look, I really like to have some audience interaction. I like to have some feedback throughout this process, so at the end of a few slides, I will pick a couple of questions that relate to what I just covered. And then at the end, we have time for everyone's Q&A." Let the audience tell you what they want.

One of the things I don't really see enough of is, when I am on a webinar, a lot of the times, I'll tailor the presentation based on the audience, and based on what I feel the audience is giving me for feedback. Many times, I'll script the slides, but then I'll go off and actually continue to drive home examples that this audience is really geared for.

After the presentation, save at least 30 minutes for the last question and answer session—this is a long one. This is after the product has been pitched and another opportunity to answer questions for a longer duration. If you're going to do any fast action bonuses, do that during this time period.

Put the time clock up there during the Q&A, and consistently bring people back to the time clock. "You've got 4 minutes left…2 minutes left…" Answer as many questions as you can. Don't say, "We're all done with questions" or "We don't have any more questions." You want people to kind of be on edge that you're getting off the call, not because there are no more questions, but because you have to do something else.

There are some questions you may not want to answer because they are about competing products, and I totally understand that. It's 100% okay to say "I don't know the answer to that question." We do a lot of search engine optimization webinars, and people often ask, "Well, what do you think about this?" You can say, "Truthfully, I don't know the answer about that particular software. I have never used it. All I know is that we have used these 3 pieces of software, and you can learn about them in our training program."

I also like to show the course on the screen: the course, the members area, the shopping cart page, the order form, all that stuff, during the Q&A section, because it really helps build trust. They know what they're getting. I will take somebody through the exact process. "You're going to go to domainname.com/sign-up and that's going to take you to this page…" That sort of transparency really means a lot, because they know exactly what they're going to get before they click the button. Oftentimes, the fear of the unknown is sometimes enough to delay purchase.

Also, be prepared, and I know I already said this, but sometimes you can get an overly idiotic customer on a webinar. You have two choices: you can either ignore them, or you can call them out. One time, there was a guest who badmouthed some screenshots that I showed, so I called him out. I wasn't trying to be a jerk, but I went into the affiliate accounts and actually started going through them, one-by-one.

Live webinars let you do a lot of awesome stuff, and when I did this, everybody on the call just seriously shut up. Some people said, "Oh my God, I'm starting to cry…" because they had been trying the affiliate marketing game for so long, and for somebody to show them the earnings shot of $8,000 or whatever…

So, two options: you can either ignore them or you can call them out.

Etiquette

In this chapter, we're going to talk about etiquette. I'm not overly huge on conforming, but I did want to have a chapter on the Dos and Don'ts of webinars, more for reference than anything else. There are things that people expect on webinars, and when you don't deliver, it hurts your brand, your reputation, and your sales.

I have had a couple clients that absolutely cannot understand that webinars are not 100% pitches. People do not get on a call with you just to hear about what it is you're offering.

Webinar Dos

Provide value. Make it worth your guests' time on the webinar. I'm anal about this. I make sure that the webinars that we put on give value, even just in the hour or two that they are on the call with us. I try to pack it with as much value as possible, so they feel good about the product, whether they bought it or not. This is my thing and I highly recommend that it be your thing as well.

Be courteous and understanding. The reason people are on the webinar is because they need help with something in their life and they've chosen you to give them that help, so be understanding.

Be prompt. Don't be late for the webinar, and if you are, apologize. Public speakers will tell you, *Don't ever apologize.* Yes, if you're running a little late, apologize. If your Internet goes down, apologize. If you've screwed up, apologize. I don't necessarily apologize for having misspellings on my PowerPoint, and, every once in a while, people will say something about it. I just tell them, "I did this presentation 20 minutes before the call, and it is not something that is scripted and edited. I want to give you as much value as possible, and I'm a Ready, Fire, Aim kind of guy."

If you have a guest, ask them if they comment a lot, or if they want you to run with the show. I always ask my co-host ahead of time, "So what are your plans for the webinar? Are you going to jump in? If not, let me know so I can start firing away."

If there are problems with the shopping cart, tell your guests that you will take care of them when you get off. So, the first webinar that we did, when we did the fast action bonuses, and just blew the doors off, there were so many people trying to get in and purchase at the same time. My server could not handle it. It was throwing weird errors, and there were people who didn't get their email sign-up stuff.

There are going to be problems. Just be clear to your attendees, and say, "Once I get off the webinar, I will take care of everything that goes into the support desk. Here's the support email and we'll get it taken care of right away." People understand.

A server going down sometimes doesn't actually even happen—it can be a ploy to make everybody believe that the demand is a lot higher than what it actually is.

If there is something that you don't know, take down the person's email and respond to them. Or, I'll be on the webinar and people asked for something, and I think, "You know what? That's an awesome addition to the training. It's not in there, but it will be."

Webinar Don'ts

Don't go from the start right into the pitch. You have to deliver value. There has to be a bonding element. People have to know who you are, where you came from, and why it matters, and they have to get some value.

Don't just leave only a few minutes for Q&A time. Do at least 15 minutes in order to make it worthwhile.

Don't be an idiot to your co-host. Most times, these are his or her people, so don't badmouth. Always be respectful of the person on the call with you, because these are his folks. They came from his or her list. They have a relationship with him or her, so make sure that you are courteous to that person.

Don't bad mouth other marketers or product owners (or their products) on the call.

Don't over-promise or under-deliver.

Don't keep people's money despite having a guarantee. If you have a guarantee, honor it.

The thing about webinars is that there is a lot of social proof and emotion, and especially if you throw in a fast action bonus, and sometimes people pull the trigger and regret it afterwards. So, make sure that if you have a guarantee, honor it. Even if with your 30-day guarantee, somebody requests a refund 40 days later, you try to figure out why it is they want a refund. Either refund them or don't. Oftentimes, we'll refund them because that's the right thing to do.

Overall, just be a good business owner!

One of the reasons webinars convert so well is because attendees are spending an hour, an hour and half with you. There's a lot of non-verbal communication just by the way your voice is inflected, or if you have video, and people pick up on things very intuitively, so be sincere.

Preparation

Webinars aren't perfect, especially when delivered live. You might be sick, you might be coughing, there might be some noise in the background. Don't worry about it.

In that fast action bonus webinar, the one that I continue to reference, the one that got 52% conversions? I coughed through the whole thing. I tried to cover it up at the mic, but sometimes I couldn't.

The Internet might cut out. Don't worry about it. Don't let it ruin your day.

Not everyone's going to be able to hear you or see your presentation, and every once in a while, you're going to see something in the question box like, "Oops! Audio just cut out!" from one person. That doesn't mean everybody can't hear you. It just means that one person can't hear you. Sometimes, there will be people left out. Again, that's just a fact of having live calls.

Sometimes, there will be nasty comments. Some people are not going to like something you say, and they will be verbal about it. There might be people deliberately trying to sabotage you in a minor way. Other product owners might be in there, trying to derail you in the middle of your presentation. That happens too. Don't let it bother you.

If you're doing it live, tell people that. Say, "I'm sorry. This isn't automated. It just kind of comes with the territory." People understand.

I also tell people that I choose to work at home, so there might be dogs in the background, or other random imperfections.

If you get bad feedback, ignore it, or try to. Or call them out. Say, "Someone in the comments just said …, and to you, I say this…"

For automated webinars, a lot of what goes on is out of your control. Obviously, you have a video recording of a webinar, so you want to make sure it is the best quality possible. You want to link to a URL, rather than talk price, so you don't have to re-record it.

You also want to answer email comments within a reasonable timeframe, usually 24 hours. Most of the automated webinar platforms will allow somebody to set a comment in via email. Also, test out the platform for a few days before you use it or mail to it, just to make sure it works.

Closing Tips

We have some really awesome tips that I want to share with you. As I mentioned, we have done plenty of webinars, and some of this is stuff that I wish somebody had told me when I started.

Webinars can be run for anything from $97 to $1,997. $497 and below as a price point is converting right now. In most markets, under $500 is what works. Also, include payment plans of 3 payments of $197. Above $497 is difficult to justify anymore without a lot of material to back up that price point, but it can be done. It depends on the product specifically.

If it is more of a coaching-oriented product, more of a one-on-one situation, yes, above $497 works. Anything above $1,997, above $2,000, need to be followed up with a call-center salesperson.

The second tip is no price on the webinar. I know I have mentioned this a few times throughout the course, but don't include a price on your PowerPoint. Let the prospect click through and see it themselves. There are advantages to that: you can do split testing; there are psychological advantages because you are letting them discover the price, and they are not hearing any weird verbal cues like you being shaky about talking about $997 price point; and lastly, you don't have to feel weird or try to justify a price verbally. You can have a short little tiny sales page that justifies the price of $997.

Third tip: Give something away. I like to try to give a flowchart or some piece of information on a webinar. I also like to get people into the sequence with a free PDF. If an affiliate is going to mail out for our webinar, the first day will offer a freely-downloadable PDF, and then, day two and day three will focus on getting them on the webinar. In order to offer the free download, post a link in the chat box. If they don't take action right away, they have a take-away piece. The people who join you on the webinar are your top action-takers. So, they will open the PDF after the webinar is done, and say, "You know what? This is a great webinar. I'm going to go back and see if it is still for sale."

The next tip is bonuses. Offer a bonus at the end of the webinar. Timed bonuses work really well—the fast action stuff. "If you buy in next 15 minutes, we'll mail you this." Also, include that in the membership area. Some people on your webinar will live outside the U.S. and there are different mail issues to send something physical in the mail. So, make sure to include whatever bonus it is in the membership area of your website.

Physical bonuses work as well, like iPads or Kindles. Offer a double or nothing: offer the course in exchange for the gift just won.

Pictures on the slides. This is something that I've tested and it seems to work pretty well, so put a picture of yourself on each slide to help with bonding. It establishes trust throughout the webinar. People continue to look at the screen with your picture, and even though you're not moving or talking, people are still a little bit more apt to purchase from you.

Put a countdown on the right sidebar, like ESPN, with the reveals of when the high points of the training will display. So, for instance, "In 12 slides, you'll learn about the #1 food that…"

Do a pitch for a strategy session. Don't include anything for sale on the webinar. Market it as *not* a sales webinar. Instead, have them sign up for a free strategy session. The sale actually takes place on the follow-up phone call. I've seen really high dollar coaching and consulting gigs fall out of this. They watch the webinar and nothing is for sale on the webinar. Where the call to action is, they say, "Go to StrategySessionSignUp.com and I will personally call you back in the next 48 hours. We will do a one-on-one strategy session, and we will get you taking action on your business." On that call follows a pitch for a $5,000 a month consulting package.

Announce buyers as they buy. This has a powerful psychological effect. "He's taking action and I want to. Since he bought, then I'm allowed to. It justifies my purchase."

Have someone manage comments for you.

Tell the audience in the question box, "If you want to get in, send a message, and we'll give you the URL." You can tell the audience about this before the bulk of the content delivery: "If you really want to be one of the first ones to get access to this, then just go ahead and type "Buy" in the question box, and we will answer with a URL where you can actually go check out this offer."

Short sales page. The URL on the webinar should be a short sales page. By short, I mean short. Just include the basics: what the product is, what it is going to do for your prospects, how to get it, and the guarantee. That's it—maybe 1,000 words at most. I try to make ours a little more personal, like, "You just sat through a 90-minute webinar for me, so I'll make this simple…" and then go from there.

The Replay

For this chapter on following up, we'll review the sequence of steps that you need to do in order to make sure that everybody who didn't attend your webinar, for whatever reason, watches a recording of the webinar.

There is a very specific autoresponder series that I send out, and we'll be covering that. We'll also be talking about some numbers so that you can scale your webinar in the next chapter.

We'll discuss the replay video, the replay autoresponder, surveys and how you can use surveys to bolster your feedback, stats and what to expect, and we'll also talk about automation.

The Webinar Replay

The replay video is one of your most powerful assets. All it is is a recording of the live webinar. You can send the link out, after the live event, to everybody who signed up for the webinar. Additionally, the people who did not attend can watch it, and you can use it in the automated webinar provider of your choice.

Some people will sign up for the live webinar just so they can get the replay and watch it later. Whether they watch it or not, is a different story. I know that I will sign up for a webinar, not to actually attend it, but so I can actually jump in and grab the replay.

There are a number of ways of recording the webinar live. If you are using GoToWebinar.com on a PC, all you have to do is login to Preferences, and Recording Options. Use the non-GoToWebinar format and it'll save to your computer. If you use the GoToWebinar format, then it won't. It will save it under a GTW codec and you don't necessarily want to have to worry about that.

On a Mac, GoToWebinar has the same the recording feature. All it is is clicking on a little button in the GoToWebinar interface. You can use a program like ScreenFlow or Camtasia to also save a copy of that webinar, so that you are double-protecting yourself.

After your webinar is done, save the webinar in its native file format, usually it's an .mp4 on a Mac, or a .wmv on a PC. Edit the webinar if you want. We usually don't edit it much, maybe the extreme beginning or the extreme end. For example, after you have hit record, before you actually go live, and you are chit-chatting with your co-host. We'll also take out the very end, as we're hunting for the Exit Webinar button.

After you get the file altogether, you can post the replay in a place that is easily accessible and viewable to the normal web-goer. If you have a YouTube account that can upload video files longer than 15 minutes, you can put it on YouTube. You can put it on SproutVideo.com, which is a video service that I really like. You can also put it on Amazon S3—it's a little more complex—but you can post it on S3, and then pool the video to your website.

Most of our replays, I put on Amazon S3. We stream the replay directly from Amazon, and then we use SproutVideo.com, which is kind of like a video repository, or an asset collection, so that we can look back through them. You never know when you're going to need them again. Also, I catalog them so that I have a lot of content to make automated webinars from.

After you upload them to the server, embed the video on a webpage somewhere. It doesn't need to be fancy—it just needs to play—either on your product site or your blog.

If it's on YouTube, make sure to embed that link on your blog. Don't mail them a link to YouTube, because there's no way for them to actually purchase your product. Underneath the video, you need to have a link that says "Click here for XYZ product," so they are able to take action. That link will then take them to the order form or the short sales pitch.

Registrant Email List Automation

Not everyone who signs up for a webinar is going to be able to make it. It's a lot worse than it used to be. Roughly 50% of signups will actually attend. Of those, only about 30% of signups will stay on through the end of the webinar. So, immediately you know that of 1,000 people who signed up, there's going to be 500 attendees, 300 will be present during the call to action, and of those, a certain percentage are going to buy. If it is a $97 product, about 30% of them are going to buy. If it is a $197 product, about 15% are going to buy, and if it's a $497 product, about 4% are going to buy.

So, if you're promoting a $97 product, roughly 900 people won't have bought; 700 people won't even know what the product is; and 500 people didn't see your presentation at all.

So, with that understanding, let's look at how you send out your post-webinar emails.

Your email series is going to be pretty boilerplate. Webinars are one of the easiest ways of building responsive email lists. The majority of people don't buy, and half don't attend, which means you have to email them with the replay link, as we talked about earlier. When they open up the email, they click the link, and they watch the replay on their own time. Use the list you generated for your webinar, import it into Constant Contact, a business-oriented email marketing provider, OfficeAutoPilot, which is by far, my favorite, or InfusionSoft, which is a lot like OfficeAutoPilot. Their features are very similar, but their email deliverability isn't quite as good.

You write up five emails that are going to go out in this specific sequence:

- **Day Zero:** Link to the replay. "Thanks so much for signing up for last night's webinar. For those of you who couldn't make it, no problem. We totally understand. Here's a link to the replay, so you can enjoy it whenever you want. So many people were asking us, before it was even over, if a replay would be available, because the content was that good…"

- **Day 1:** Link to the replay again. "Did you miss yesterday's link? Or maybe you just wanted to take some extra notes? Here's a link to the replay from a few days ago. It's coming down in 72 hours, though. Just so you know—it's a beast on our servers."

- **Day 2:** Link to the replay AND link to the order form. "If you're reading this, you haven't bought yet. We really wanted to make sure you saw the video; we wanted to make sure you saw the product; so, here's the link to the webinar replay and here's the link to the product. We assume you've already watched the video, so I didn't want to make you go re-watch the video in order to get the link to the shopping cart."

- **Day 3:** Link to the replay AND link to the order form again. "Tomorrow is the last day. Make sure you grab your bonuses… Bonuses are expiring… You are covered by the guarantee… If you want to take action, you only have a little bit longer to do it… Here's a link to the replay. Here is a link to the product."

- **Day 4:** Link to the order form. "Last chance for the bonuses… We're pulling the replay… This is the last time you'll be able to take notes… Here's a link to the product order form."

If they don't purchase within five days, then they are probably not going to, at least not in this particular sequence.

So, what now? You had a webinar and you tried to get them to purchase something on the webinar. You sent them five days worth of emails, and you continually prodded them to purchase your product. After those five days of emails, what happens? What do you do?

Sometimes, affiliates like to put it in their autoresponder. They like to put this whole sequence in their autoresponder, so they continue to send traffic to this webinar. People are going to come back to the webinar for the training. You may get some sales to trickle in, but it's not for sure.

You can also do a trial offer. You can say, "On the webinar, the price was $97. Since you haven't bought yet, price may be an issue, and that's totally understandable. So, what we're going to do is offer a trial for $4.95, and then in 14 days, we're going to rebill the rest. So, there will be an additional payment of $97, but you're going to be able to test out the product for 14 days before you have to actually pay."

Make sure they pay more on the trial that if they had taken the initial offer. You don't want people to feel slighted, like all of a sudden, you are offering a discount, if they are perhaps still on that email list. Don't give them the bonuses, if any were offered. You don't want to make it more advantageous for them to purchase on a trial when you just had a five-day scarcity window.

Mail the next offer in your pipeline. That's the beauty of webinars. Sure, you will make some money up front, but they are beautiful for building a good list.

After your five-day replay sequence, and if you decided to put a trial offer in for a couple days, mail the next affiliate offer. Mail the next offer in your product lineup. Do another webinar for another product.

Typically, if people signed up for one webinar, they are going to sign up for more. Webinar-goers are repetitive—they like webinars. Look around for other webinars that are converting in your market, and then ask to be an affiliate of those, and mail to those.

Feedback

Let's talk about surveys, and how you can use surveys to get some great feedback about your webinar and about your product.

One of my favorite things to do after a webinar is survey the attendees. You can survey immediately or you can survey through the autoresponder, both buyers and prospects.

Surveys are huge in information marketing. You can collect incredible feedback that can be used for making better products, having great testimonials, or making future products.

There are a couple of different times I like to send surveys:

Immediately after the webinar: GoToWebinar. has an interesting feature that lets you survey people immediately after the webinar. No one uses it! When you exit the webinar, it pops up a survey on your desktop, and you can either fill it out or not. However, you will get a lot of response to this survey, because people feel obliged because you just gave them great content. You just sat on the phone with them for over an hour.

Here's how you set it up: After you create the webinar, go to Surveys in the drop-down link above the webinar, and click it. You can then add up to 10 questions.

We use 4 questions:
- Did you like the call?
- What was your biggest take-away?
- What can we do better?

- Overall, what did you think? (This is for testimonials).
- Each of those questions has a little text box that allows them to enter a couple sentences.

After each webinar, read through the answers and use them as you see fit. Use them to change up your webinar content; use them to change up the product or the pitch.

Don't let one person derail you. Don't let one person's response set you off and have you totally change your marketing angle. However, if you see a common theme, then think about working it in your webinar.

Another opportunity for surveys is after somebody buys. After somebody buys, survey them. Ask them why they bought. What was the reason they bought? What did they like about the product that made them buy? What was the feature or benefit that stuck out for them?

Email them a link to a Google Docs form asking them what problem are they are they specifically looking to solve? What are you hoping the course will do for you personally? What are your desired outcomes? This helps anchor those emotions and outcomes in them, so that they take the course more seriously and are committed to it. It gives you great feedback because you know why people bought, and you can use that in your sales messages, and make them even more potent than they already are.

If somebody doesn't buy, ask them why not. Somebody goes through your sequence, your webinar, or your replay sequence, ask them why not. Why didn't you buy? Was there something you were looking for that wasn't there? Was a problem with the video or the order form?

You'll be amazed at what you find out. People will tell you why they didn't buy. Sometimes they can be a little bit nasty, but overall, it gives great feedback, and shows you things that you didn't know were actually happening.

Metrics

Let's talk about webinar stats. Getting into numbers can get a little dry, but I really want you to pay attention to these.

Here are normal attendee stats:

The signup page is going to get about 35% conversion. That means that 35 out of 100 people coming to your signup page are actually going to sign up for your webinar.

The next stat is webinar sales conversion rate. These are the numbers that you want to try to target and hit of the people who are actually coming to your webinar. So, if it's a $97 product price, you want roughly 30% of your attendees to purchase that product. If the product price is $197, you want roughly 15% to buy the product. If the price is $497, you want roughly 4% to buy. Anything above these numbers is extraordinary, and you have a really hot webinar that you really need to continue scaling.

If your conversions are off, lower than what you see, then tweak your webinar every time you do it to try to increase them.

Another 4% to 9% are going to purchase your product because of the replay. The lower the price point, the higher the conversion. So, 4% for $497 and 9% for $97. The ratio is a little bit off, and one of the reasons is because when you pitch a $497 product, they have to think about it another couple of days.

So, here's how we would look at it actually detailed out:

- 3,500 people see the webinar Sign-Up Page
- 1,000 people actually sign up
- 500 attendees
- 300 are present during the Call to Action
- Of those, a certain percentage buy:
  - $97 – 30% or 90 buyers
  - $197 – 15% or 45 buyers
  - $497 – 4% or 12 buyers

After the webinar:

- 910 people are emailed the replay link. Those are the people who did not buy.
- 200 people click the link
- 18 more people buy

This is how everything will shake out:

- A Total of 108 buyers
- 892 prospects that you can mail the additional offers to

This is assuming a $97 price point. These numbers are absolutely for explanation only.

All in all, that means 108 buyers and 892 prospects out of 1000 people who sign up for your webinar. This yields to a pretty interesting set of metrics:

Earnings per attendees (EPA) - Every attendee on your webinar is worth X amount of money.

Earnings per click (EPC) - Every click going to your webinar signup page is worth X amount of money.

EPCs and EPAs are industry-accepted metrics that you can use to get affiliates to promote a webinar for you.

Using these numbers from the previous slide, this is how you breakdown your earnings:

Earnings Per Click:

- 3,500 visitors (or clicks)
- 108 buyers X $97 price point = $10,476.00 revenue
- $10,476 / 3,500 = $2.99 EPCs – this means for every click you get onto your signup page, you are going to make $2.99.

Earnings Per Attendee:
- $10,476 / 500 attendees = $20.95 per attendee – this means for every person you can get on your webinar, you are going to make $20.95.

Affiliates love these numbers, because they know they can get 1,000 clicks, which means they'll make $2,990. If they can get ten attendees, they are going to make $209.50. If they get 100 attendees, they will make $2,095.

That's why these numbers are important.

Your goal in order to make it worthwhile for affiliates, or banner advertising, is to have a greater than $2 EPC and a greater than $16 EPA.

Your goal:

- EPCs > $2
- EPAs > $16

If you have better numbers than that, any affiliate will promote you. They understand these numbers.

These numbers are huge for growing your webinar business.

Webinar Automation

Once you get the stats from your webinar, the EPAs and the EPCs will give you numbers to work with to automate the whole process.

How much do you have to spend to make money? That's the question you have to ask yourself.

Here are our numbers:

- Earnings Per Click = $2.99.
- Earnings Per Attendee = $20.95.

If you spend less than $2.99 per click, you're making money.

If you spend less than $20.95 to get somebody on the webinar, you're making money.

This is just dollars and cents stuff that allows you to do a lot of interesting things:

- Pay-per-click or Adwords
- Banner Ads, such as using SiteScout.com or BuySellAds.com
- Affiliate marketing

As long as you're spending less than $2.99 per click, you're golden—you can send as much traffic as you want.

This is where automated platforms really come in. Driving traffic to webinars that happen without you actually having to be there is the name of the game. All you need is email marketing—you've got that. You need successful webinar replay—you've got that, too. All you need is traffic. So, anything less than \$2.99 per click is where you want to be.

That is the key to building a successful business: spending less than you're making. With automation, you can scale this as high as you want.

Scaling With Webinars

Let's talk about what you need to do to scale your business outside of just one webinar, or a couple of webinars, and actually turn it into a huge six- or seven-figure business. We're going to talk about how to scale webinars, how to turn one webinar into an entire business, review some cautions, and then some next steps.

The Million-Dollar Webinar

Every once in a while, you'll hear about somebody doing a million-dollar webinar. The premise behind it is really pretty simple and it's stuff you already know how to do. You create a webinar that sells a product, you test it, you figure out the numbers, the EPCs and the EPAs, and then you send traffic with PPC and banners, affiliates, and email solo ads.

This isn't necessarily a paid-traffic book, but this is what you need to do in order to tip the scales. What I will do is walk through and give you a bunch of tips on each of them.

Here is how pay-per-click works.

There are a couple of different ad platforms that we like to use. One is Google Adwords, and it uses either their search network or their content network. The search network allows you to place ads in Google properties, like Google.com, along their right sidebar, and Google Maps and YouTube, anything that Google owns.

Next is the content network. Google has done a masterful job of allowing bloggers and website owners to display Google ads for them, and then they get a cut of whatever revenue Google collects from clicks on those ads. So, I highly advise you use the content network, and create some simple ugly banner.

Surprisingly, ugly banners get higher click-through rates. Basically, create an ad with a white background, red headline, maybe an image, black text, blue link, really ugly stuff. They tend to have a really great click-through rate. The better the click-through rate, the cheaper traffic you will be able to send.

Another network we like to use is BuySellAds.com. BuySellAds.com is a banner advertising service. You can go there, sign up as an advertiser, and then you're able to place ads on any of the sites in their network. All you have to do just find a site in your niche, buy a couple of banner ad spots, upload your creative, and send traffic back to your automated webinar signup page.

You can also use SiteScout.com. They have a retargeting campaign, and you can also place banners on thousands of sites across a whole bunch of different networks. It is a really great tool to use. They have training tutorials on how to use them, but again, it's another awesome resource.

Probably the easier option, rather than paid advertising, is going out to find affiliates. So a few tips on finding affiliates: The first and probably the easiest thing to do is find a JV broker. This is more advanced and more about networking, but whenever you hear about a JV broker, follow them on Facebook and Twitter.

There are different JV brokers for different niches. Basically, he or she knows a bunch of people who all have products that help promote each other. A lot of times, he will arrange a reciprocal promotion between you and that product owner. The other product owner promotes you and you promote that other product owner. The JV broker gets a cut in the middle. They get 10% either way. Some JV brokers are better than others, but finding affiliates is a bulletproof way of scaling a business.

Another way that we really like to do it is to reach out to people ranking in the search engines for the keywords relevant to your product. So, if you have a health and fitness offer, a dieting offer, go ahead and Google *foods to lose weight* and reach out to the site owners. Offer to do a guest post, offer to buy a banner on the website, or offer to pay them to put a text link on their site and send traffic back to your automated webinar.

Another thing we like to do is find leaderboards from products launching in the markets that we're in and we contact those affiliates. So, if there is a big product launch, and it lists the top 20 affiliates for that product, which most big launches will do, because there are affiliate prizes, we'll reach out on Facebook, LinkedIn, and their blog, to see if they want to promote your product. The idea is that they promoted somebody else's product and probably made a bunch of money, so they can make a bunch of money with you and your product. We call this leaderboard sniping.

We also like to do solo ads. We will pay somebody to mail their list of 20,000 to 30,000 people. If you go to WarriorForum.com, and look in the broker section, there are people who post solo ads. "Give me $250 to mail to my list of 10,000. You'll get a thousand clicks." It's pretty cheap advertising.

Another option we will use is at SRDS.com. You can sign up for an account for $800, and it's all the businesses that have listed customers. You can work with those businesses to get them to mail your email out to their list.

You can also search Google for relevant sites and asked for a mailing in exchange for money. We call this the solo-sniper method. You just go to Google and type {niche} + "powered by aweber.com." Your niche, for example, can be *gardening* and aweber.com is an email marketing platform. What you're going to find is thousands of results for people who are building a list around your category or niche. It's a great way of finding some under-the-radar solo ads that you're able to go and market through.

From A Single Webinar Into An Empire

In this chapter, we're going to discuss building a business around your webinar.

Once you get a converting webinar on the books, figure out what else people want. What can you sell them that makes their experience a little better? What allows them to give you more money? This is called upsells and downsells.

Figure out what people want who don't buy. The prospects who don't buy the first time may still be buyers, but just not for your product, or for your first product. Maybe they are waiting for something that's a little bit better-suited to them, or they are waiting for some affiliate product that you can introduce them to.

An upsell is something that you can add after the initial sale that is going to benefit the buyer. It's not necessarily packaged in with the initial product, but you can offer to them directly afterwards. An upsell might be software, any additional or related training, or maybe downloads, PDFs, graphics, stuff that makes the original product easier or better. This is not to say that you need to devalue the original product. Just figure out what else they want and give it to them.

A downsell happens when you present an upsell, and the buyer doesn't take it. After they purchase, they finish in the shopping cart, and then they hit an upsell page. "Thanks so much for buying XYZ product. We know that a lot of people who purchase the same product you did also really like this particular add-on. So, we are offering it to you at a special discount." That is an upsell.

If they decline that upsell, then you can send them to a downsell. "We know you just declined. We know that you didn't want to take {the upsell}, so what we're going to do is offer you the same product at a 50% discount, just as a fast action bonus, or just as a one-time offer. All you have to do is click the Add To Cart button below to get started." That's a downsell.

There are a few ways to position downsells that are easy. You can break the upsell down into payment plans. You can give a discount on the downsell, or you can add something to the upsell, or make a physical version of the product itself. You can say, "Okay, so you turned us down for the for the e-book. What if we send you the book in the mail. It's only going to be $10 more." The only time people see downsells is if they don't take the upsells, so you don't have to worry about people feeling slighted about discounts on something they already purchased.

Sometimes a downsell is the same product in a different format or limited version. If someone passed on buying your physical course that is a box full of DVDs and workbooks, the downsell could be the same content in online form. If someone said no to your software with an unlimited license, the downsell could be a license limiting the use to one user or on one website.

People who don't buy your initial offer are still good buyers. Maybe it just didn't affect them the way you wanted it to. What kinds of affiliate products sell? Can you recreate those? Are you able to send them to an affiliate's product, maybe as a different spin on the same thing? Survey them and figure out what they want. They are going to tell you and then they'll buy from you.

This is one of my favorite ways of creating new products: surveying our customer list and asking "What do you want to learn more about?" They will tell us that they want more information about _____. Then we will create that, and oftentimes, we will give them that for free, since they were kind in telling us what they wanted. Then we can use them as a beta test for a product.

Webinar Warnings

Scaling a business is all about the numbers, so if you can purchase leads for less than they're worth, it's good business. You can scale to the moon.

If you can purchase a lead for $1, and make $2 off that lead, then you are doubling your money. So why wouldn't you spend every last cent you had to double your money? If you find yourself spending more per lead than the EPCs of your webinar, either build out a longer autoresponder sequence, or add in more upsells or downsells. It is really pretty much the easiest thing to do.

When buying traffic, it's easy to spend $5,000 to $50,000 per month, so know your numbers. If you spend $50,000 to make $70,000, that's a good deal. If you're negative—if you spent $50,000 to only make $30,000, you have to figure out how to get that money back.

Please don't fall prey to coaching floors if you don't have to. Coaching floors are where they will call a prospect, and try to sell them at $10,000 coaching package. Don't do that unless you have to. I highly recommend against it. It's easy using webinars and automating webinars to break even pretty early on. Just make sure you have a good upsell and downsell mix, and you should be good to go.

Don't beat up your list either. Don't send offer after offer. Give value between affiliate promotions, so, send them to blog posts, create videos for your folks, or do how-to stuff for free with tutorials and stuff on your blog.

Just make sure to keep your list current—it's your number one asset! Make sure they keep clicking links, because if they don't click links, you don't make money.

Next Steps

Hopefully, you have been actively creating your webinar as you're going through this section of the book: getting the software, putting together the presentation, getting it scheduled, etc.

The next step is really making sure that your presentation is dialed in. Make sure you're getting the best EPCs and EPAs you can. Once you get some good EPCs, as we talked in the stats chapter, you need to start sending traffic to these webinars.

After that, figure out your numbers, put together a clear plan on scaling, and reach for the moon.

There's no reason why you can't have a multimillion dollar webinar, too. If you follow even half of what's in this book, you're going to be able to. You have to have a great product, whether you're a digital product owner or a local business or somebody who sells widgets, it doesn't matter, you can still use webinars to sell your products. You just want to make sure that the webinar is converting to a level that you can send more traffic to.

Go back through this book. There are nuggets in here that you're only going to pick up after you do some webinars. There are things in this book that I that I took for granted, and now I'm putting together procedures based on this course for our stuff. We run hundreds of webinars and this is the very best stuff I know to do, so take it seriously.

With webinars, you don't need to know sales copy. That's the beautiful thing—just telling a story and pitching your product is really all you need to do.

PART FOUR – SALES COPY

Copywriting

The sales copy is the most important thing on your website, because it's actually what is going to make you money. This part of the book is dedicated entirely to the sales copy and writing to sell products. The idea behind it is that your website is live 24 hours a day. You want to be able to sell a product any time, day or night. Having well-written sales copy keeps that going.

Sales copy poses an interesting challenge. You need to actually sell something to somebody through text, audio, or video. You can't sell it face-to-face, so there isn't a language connection or facial expression to go off of. If you sell something face-to-face, you can read body language and facial expression to see what and how people might be thinking. You can't do that online, which means your copy has to be emotional and logic based.

Picture your ideal buyer. Think about what they do when they wake up, what they have for breakfast, what kind of car they drive, how big their family is, how much money they make, where they live, what they do for a living, and anything else you can think of. You have to know and understand your prospect's wants, fears and desires. So when you think about what they want, you need to go deeper than what they tell their spouse they want, or what they should want. You have to ask yourself, what is it, at the core of their being, do they want? Do they want to be free? Financially stable? To drive a Lamborghini? Find out.

When you think about their fears, what are they afraid of? Are they afraid of being broke or disappointing someone? Think about their desires. Think about what they want more than anything else, their deepest desires. When you know the answers, they you're going to be able to write proper sales copy for them. You need to know their possible objections and pinpoint why boundaries don't matter. You need to speak conversationally with them and put yourself in their situation. Imagine what their reactions will be when they read your sales copy.

You should understand that they will be looking for reasons to say no and they will find mistakes to reassure themselves. They're actually going to pick apart what you're saying and what they're reading. They won't want to believe it's actually them you're talking about. You have to think about the reason they are on your page to begin with, and tap into that. You can easily tell them that they have permission to say no to you, make it clear that they have a choice. Bring it to their level and say "Look, I think you'll be interested in this. You might not be, and if you aren't, that's fine. But, if you give me a minute, I can tell you how to live a life free of panic attacks. If you're interested, keep reading. If it's not for you, that's okay too."

Traditional direct response copy emphasizes conversion rates and squeezing every last cent out of the buyer. That's not necessarily a good thing, in my opinion. I don't like the fact that video sales letters and direct response marketers are so psychologically keyed in and use neurolinguistic programming. They are so keyed in that they will stop at nothing to get a sale. They look at conversion rates and say "I need to have a 4% conversion rate or else it's a failure." It's not true, because you might be able to manage a 2% conversion rate and then another 1.5% comes later. Gary Vee actually spoke at a ClickBank Exchange, which I attended, about leaving the table. He said "I leave 20% on the table every day, but they buy eventually. He leaves sales on the table, but people come back every day and watch his show and end up buying something from him eventually. That is why we build email lists and market, so people can make the choice to buy from us eventually.

Logistically, there are two types of sales letters. There are video sales letters, and there are long copy sales letters, which we have told you about previously. Video sales letters are again, PowerPoint presentations where you actually just read the text that's on the slide, and long copy sales letters are very long, often with lots of images. A lot of the time, they're anywhere between 10 and 20 pages typed. Moderate and long copy sales letters are heavily graphic based, so there are a lot of graphics, images, fonts, and attention grabbers. They don't easily convert into video sales letters now, so fewer people are using long copy sales letters. They still work, and they can also be used in a way that video sales letters cannot, which is sent through the mail.

We'll get to the video sales letter later on. The next few chapters will cover the essentials of the long copy sales letters, the headline, problem, solution, credibility, product information, guarantee, price, close, and intensifiers. If you're looking at a long copy sales letter, this is the exact template it will follow. All you have to do is fill in the sections and you'll have a fantastic sales letter.

Headlines

The first part of our sales letter is the headline. Headlines are the first thing that people see and they are a critical part of the whole sales page and letter. It's usually in red or blue color at the top of the page. There has been a lot of testing on both color headlines, and both work pretty well at drawing attention. In a sales video, the headline is the first slide of that PowerPoint. It will need to be manufactured or massaged to evoke an emotion from your crowd. It will need to allude to the product and convey the benefits of the product itself.

You can use any of these examples to apply to your headline. So "Cutting-Edge _____ Reveals Ten Easy Tricks to _____."

Fill it in and you have "Cutting-Edge Marketing Software Reveals Ten Easy Tricks to Make Money Online." Or, "Cutting-Edge Greenhouse Plan Reveals Quick Ways You Can Set Up in Your Backyard for under $100." Something like that.

Another example is "Breakthrough Formula Reveals _____."

So, "Breakthrough Formula Reveals Nature's Number One Way of Harvesting Energy." Or, "Breakthrough Formula Reveals Number One Secret Behind Low-Emission Fuel."

You can even play off of prospects themselves, like "Broke, Depressed Housewife Discovers Secret Blueprint to Make Money While Staying Home." Or, "Broke, Depressed Housewife Discovers Secret Blueprint to Get Her Kids to Behave for the Summer." You get the idea. Sometimes all you have to do is fill in the blanks. You won't get the headline right on the first try, but you can test them out. Some great copywriters use 10, 20, or even 50 different tries to get the headline right. Your first go-around doesn't need to have that much effort put into it, but you'll get the hang of it and find what suits you.

You can also split test. Split testing or A/B testing is going to show that you can get 50% or so more sales from a headline change. Split testing is where you take two different versions of a sales letter, and split traffic to each one. It is a very good way to know which version of your sales letter is working better due to a headline. A useful tool for split testing is VisualWebsiteOptimizer.com. Google also has a split testing tool called Website Optimizer. It isn't super reliable though. We have run tests on the results, and the metrics just don't quite stack up. Visual Website Optimizer is a great platform. You can set up split tests for free, and if you want to get more versions of split testing, it's a cheap monthly fee.

Split testing is going to compare different pages, promotions, prices and whatever else you want to compare, and you can actually figure out the best price based on what is selling and where the traffic is. You can set up so that if you have four of the same sales letters, each with a different headline, the Optimizer tool will direct 25% of traffic to each site, and then compare results to see which page converts better.

All the headline is going to do is interest prospects enough to make them read the content below it. That is how sales pages are manufactured, with the intent to get the prospect to read the next line and keep going. It's the same with a video sales letter also; you just want to keep the prospect's attention on the next slide.

If your copy works well, people just keep reading right down the page and they're presented with all the information they need in order to make a buying decision. Then they hit the purchase price, hit the "Add to cart" button, and purchase your next product. No one will read just the headline alone and immediately purchase your product. But they will read the headline and keep reading, and that's the biggest benefit of having a good one.

The Problem

The next section in your sales letter, after the headline, is the problem. The problem is where you present what it is that the prospect is there for. You want to identify what they are experiencing, what it is that they are having a problem with. Every digital product is a solution for something, so you want to make sure you're really identifying the problem to get them to buy the solution. People are at your site because they have found your headline reveals that you have an answer. Use the problem section to really bond with your prospect. If people can feel that you have experienced what they have, then they keep reading.

That is why it is so important that you see the problem through your prospect's eyes. Think about when you broke up with a boyfriend or girlfriend. Maybe it's a song that makes you sad, or driving past a restaurant you two frequented is upsetting. There are common elements across everybody who has been through a breakup; it's just a fact of human nature. The problem is going to be relevant to the story behind it. If the prospect hasn't been through what it is you're describing as the problem, they probably wouldn't visit your site in the first place.

It is a unique kind of pain that you can key into in your sales copy, and every problem has that kind of pain. You need to actually find out what it is they are feeling, and try to understand what you may be doing to get through it. It's going to make the prospect understand that you know what it's like to be where you're and it will bond you to your prospect. If they realize that you know what you're talking about and you have figured out an answer, they will keep reading.

Posing the problem in the form of a story is a must. You can even begin with "I'm going to tell you a story." People love stories because they break them of their trance and existence, if even for a short time. People love living life through others, hence the popularity of reality TV shows. How many hours do people spend watching television about the lives of others, simply because it is entertaining? People like seeing drama unfold, and it makes us feel more normal. If you're posing the problem, you better believe that people think you have the solution, or why talk about it at all? You want to make it strong and believable. Only after you write about pain, worries, and tragedy are prospective buyers going to buy your product. That will help you write a conversational, high-converting sales copy. The problem itself needs to be as long or as short as you need in order to actually convey that you know what you're talking about. The problem moves right into the solution, and you'll end up pointing right to the product.

The problem itself needs to - it can be however long or short you need in order to actually convey that you know what it is you're talking about. Up next we're going to talk about the solution. The problem is going to move right into the solution. So you're going to pose the problem, you're going to talk about all the pain and heartache that this person has felt and you have felt in going through the same situation. And then you're going to move right into the solution. The solution is what you've found that has helped ease the pain of the problem. And then from the solution you move into the product.

The Solution

After you have posed the problem, present the solution. It is a natural tendency to move into the solution after you have shown the prospect the problem. You want to begin to talk about your prospect getting out of their rut and leaving the pain associated with the problem behind. You have successfully convinced the prospect that you know what they are going through and what it feels like to be on the other side after you have found the solution. You then need to tell them what it feels like to have actually conquered the problem that you posed and start giving them hope. Talk about how you were able to pick yourself up by the bootstraps and come up with the solution. Talk about all of the good things that came out of the solution.

You want to go into detail about the struggle and the length of time it took to get to the solution. This will start to pre-frame your audience into the product. Go into detail about what steps you took. Did you actually sit down and write a list of steps and action items and go through them? Or, maybe you woke up one day and had this sudden realization of a way that you could get past the problems you faced. Maybe it was easy, maybe it was extremely hard. Talk about how much mental effort it took to do the steps you had to take to get where you are now. Talk about revelations, thinking clearly, and your expectations. Let your readers know what you expected to come out of the process, and what you thought of the process itself.

One thing you can do to get into posing a solution, is ask yourself what other people think about you as a result of the process. If you can find out what other's views are on what you accomplished, you can get a good idea of how prospects want to feel after a successful solution. You want to help people see the aftermath of the problem they are facing, what it feels like to be better, and how to get there.

The solution is ideally going to be story based. The idea is you had a problem, you found a way to overcome it, and now you want to change the world by revealing your solution. You need to make your prospects feel that you really want to give them the solution to their problem.

Be sure to include social proof or what other people think about you as a result. It can be Facebook comments, emails, testimonials, anything that shows prospects that you have already helped others. You want to transition from the story, then the solution, and then into credibility all in story form. It all needs to be emotion based. You're engaging the emotional side of the brain, not the logical side of the brain. You can do so by telling stories, and the logistical bit will come later.

Credibility

In this section, we'll talk about credibility. Before engaging with you, or buying from you, people want to know they can trust you. They want to know that you have an answer to their problem and that they are safe with you. They want to feel assured that they are safe giving you money, listening to you, and safe to invest the mental energy it will take to implement the solution in their lives.

Credibility is all about proof. It isn't about education, degrees, or certifications. Some people are really caught up in all that, but it doesn't matter. In a sales letter, it isn't going to matter what degree you have. You need to have a certain amount of credibility in your language and stories in order for people to actually understand that you know what it is that they are going through. It's really about the language itself. You can have a picture of a diploma in your sales letter, but your prospects are not going to bond to it, they'll bond to you.

Take Tony Robbins, for example. He isn't certified, nor does he have a degree in leadership or psychology or anything that he teaches, but he's one of the most influential people in the world. Credibility can be you on stage, a snapshot of your ClickBank account, a picture of you teaching a group of people, a picture of you before and after you lost 70 pounds, or a picture of you and your ex together again. Whatever it is you're trying to gain credibility for, show your prospects you have been there, and you'll gain their trust. You can include testimonials from previous customers who are satisfied with your product. The testimonials for you and your product can be in video, photo, or text form, basically anything that attributes some of the success that person has had to you and your product.

The goal of putting up these testimonials is to get prospects picturing the results they'll have if they work with you. You want somebody else to picture themselves in that Ferrari they've dreamed about or enjoying the same rewards that you've been enjoying. You want prospects to envision the results and the life that you've created for yourself. All in all, you want them to put themselves in your shoes after they've solved the problem they've been facing. You want them to bask in the idea of having solved or rectified that problem.

The social element and the testimonials offer proof that what you do works for people. Proof gives prospects the ability to trust you and to really feel safe buying from you. You want them to think about all of the people who are already satisfied with your product. If you can offer a ton of testimonials and proof that what you offer works, you're going to have a lot of success selling your product. Making those prospects part of the vision of the overall success of your product is a really important part of the process. It should go without saying, don't fake credibility or testimonials. It's better to have no testimonial at all rather than faked testimonials. The U.S. Federal Trade Commission has really put an end to fake testimonials. They put a lot of regulations out that have come down hard on testimonials and case studies, and you actually need to have documentation on each and every testimonial you use.

Besides testimonials, you're going to need to provide some proof that you know what you're talking about. Credibility doesn't have to come in the form of a testimonial. Credibility can be in social proof, like the fact that you have 2,200 likes on your Facebook page, audio recordings of your product or reviews, even pictures. A simple way to earn this credibility is to even create it yourself. All you really have to do is email educational content and how-to information about your process and product. You can then ask those prospects to buy from you, and the credibility is kind of implied. You've already established the credibility because what you're sent them is already working. It's simple yet brilliant.

In the next few chapters we are going to get into more product information. The entire process builds upon each section of the product and the whole picture will come together as we work through it.

The Offer

The product information begins the introduction to what you have actually created. We are going to jump away from the story of you and your problem, solution, credibility, and all of the other stuff we just went over. We want to get into the fact that you have actually created something that is going to solve this prospect's problem. There are some important factors you're going to want to cover in order to properly introduce your product. You'll need to talk about what your product is, its name, and what it solves.

Go into detail about what your product does. Break down the steps of the plan. Talk about the different chapters and why it's broken down the way it is. Talk about the features and benefits of the product. The features and benefits section will probably be the largest of the product information space, but it needs to be created in a certain way. You need to go into detail about how it's delivered. Is it a physical product or a digital product? Is it a video product that people actually log into and watch the videos on their computer? Quantify your product. Make sure your prospect knows is has eight hours of video or 46 pages.

You'll usually just be able to list out individual sections because it will commonly be descriptive enough to identify what the chapters contain. You'll also want to include any covers or digital box shots to illustrate your product. If you have any ecovers of virtual DVDs created that actually show the digital product itself, use them. You can get those created on outsourcing sites like Fiverr for a low price. You should explain what your product does and why it is critical to have it. What does your buyer get from your product? How does it tie in to their problem and solution? How does it achieve their desired result?

Features and benefits are an important part of your copy. A feature is something specific about your product. For instance, a chapter covering the specific letter you write to your ex to get them back is a feature. The benefit is what happens because you wrote that letter, it always happens because of the feature. You can also include the feature and benefit together, like "Included is a letter template so your ex comes running back to you, totally forgetting why they left and why they were mad at you in the first place. That's one feature-benefit statement.

One of the biggest mistakes people make when writing copy is to talk about just the features rather than the benefits. Airbags on a car are a feature; the benefit is they protect you and your family in a crash.

You'll end up having many of these feature-benefit statements, and they need to pinpoint the critical points of the product to your prospect. You'll find that someone will pay $37 for just that template letter to get their ex back. Those people won't read everything, but they will email your support saying "Where in your product is this specific feature and benefit?" That will be the only reason they purchased your product. The features and benefits are really strong. They are going to be what really sells your product.

Make sure your prospect is aware of how your product is delivered. The answer to that should be easy; it's either shipped to them, downloaded, or accessed online. If it's digital, how? Is it live, a members-only area, or a webinar? Let your prospects know if they'll get further access on your website and a login or password. You want them to be as comfortable as possible with what happens after they actually buy your product. If they enter their credit card information and purchase your product, what happens then? Are they taken to a specific page that guides them through the start of use of your product? They trust that they will be taken to the right location to begin using your product, but what happens if they are not? Explain to them exactly what will happen when they purchase. Will they be taken to a download page? Will a link be emailed to them? Will something be shipped to them?

The easiest way to do this is to tell them upfront what to expect after purchase. You can go into detail about product fulfillment and what to expect after the sale. Something like "After you purchase the product, you'll get immediate access to the members-only section" works fine. You want to list whatever it is your product includes and quantify it. It will help them envision the product so that they can start to talk themselves into it and question how they are going to keep on living without it.

The Guarantee

A guarantee is definitely necessary in your sales copy. New vendors or product owners are hesitant to offer a guarantee on their material because they are afraid that people will ask for their money back, especially with digital products. The fact is, people will ask you for refunds whether you offer a guarantee or not. With a guarantee on your product, you'll sell about three times more than without it. Legally, all 50 states give a buyer 30 days guarantee anyway, whether you have it listed in your sales copy or not.

A guarantee is going to make your prospects feel safe. It's going to help position you as a good guy that prospects will take a chance on because you'll refund them their money. You'll also see that competition in your market will offer a guarantee. It may seem like it's a bad idea, but it doesn't mean that all your buyers are going to take you up on it. By having a guarantee, your refund rate increases by about 2%. But, you're selling about three times more product, so the conversion is worth it. We'll go through digital product and physical product refund rates also.

You can get creative with your guarantees. ClickBank has a mandatory 60-day money-back guarantee, which is fine if you're going through them. If you're adamant that your product is worth it, you can do a six-month guarantee, a one-year guarantee, or even a lifetime guarantee. If you can prove that the metrics of your product work, you can throw in an "everything but the kitchen sink or triple your money back" guarantee. Crazy, but worthwhile if you stand behind your product.

You're unfortunately still going to encounter people that want their money back, even after the guarantee period. It sucks, but it's still your call whether or not to give it to them. There are some people that are adamant about it, and even on day 47 after a 30 day guarantee has expired, they'll come to you and say "I want my money back," and they'll be persistent about it. In situations like that, I encourage you to refund the money because with all of the social media available to the prospects, they can easily exploit you or your product. You really don't want to give someone a reason to give you a bad name through social media. Just make sure your prospects are happy.

You're apt to encounter those unhappy buyers who want a refund. Sometimes in those situations, you may have already paid an affiliate for the sale. After the 30 day refund period has expired, you pay the affiliate. If you have a $497 product, after those 30 days are up, you pay the affiliate the 50% or whatever the rate is. So the affiliate makes their $250, but now your buyer wants a full refund. If you explain the situation to your buyer, sometimes you can offer them the half of a refund and they'll accept. If you refund them their entire $497, you've just gone in the hole for $250. You can respond to them by reiterating the 30 day guarantee, and telling them you've already paid the affiliate, saying you can no longer offer a refund. If they persist about the refund, usually an offer of half, or whatever it is you made off of the sale is sufficient enough for them not to press the issue further

In general, the digital product refund rate is usually about 15%. Physical products have a refund rate of about 7-8%. A book, video course, or anything like that has a much lower refund rate but it's also more difficult to get set up and fulfilled. ClickBank actually started to charge vendors as a penalty to get their refunds under 15%. Since a lot of those vendors make money with online products, they have refund rates of 30%, 35%, or even 40%. There are issues with refunds, so you want to try and keep yours as low as possible.

There are some customer retention strategies that you can dive into if refunds get to be a problem. You can offer half of the money back, or you can tie in some physical products as well. In order for them to actually get the refund they want, they have to send their physical product back to you, which can cost them some shipping and handling as well. There are quite a few ways you can get customers to stay with you, but you always want to make sure you have their best interest at heart because everyone does have a voice, and that can eventually tarnish your product or name.

If they ask for a refund, give it. If it's after the refund period, then tread lightly. It's really the best advice I can give. By having a guarantee, you're going to be making a lot more money.

The Close

The close of the sales letter can be done with three big points within your sales copy in order to have the best effect. The first is the emotional close. The emotional close is everything that isn't necessarily concrete. It is your story, the problem, fears, likes, dislikes, hopes, and desires. All of that is emotional. Second is logic. You're going to have everything that is fact-based. You want to include the numbers, pricing, money-back guarantee, analytics and results, processes, etc. Remind your prospects that when this happens, this is the result. Give a short statement on those features and benefits with results. Lastly, there's fear based information. It's mostly about the scarcity of what may happen without the product.

In a sales letter, the problem, solution, and product information are all emotional. You're trying to tell stories and get the prospect to envision themselves after conquering the problem. Once you have introduced the price, you're giving them the ability to buy your product. Up until that first price point, that process is all emotional. At this point, some will buy your product without even delving into the logic of it. Not many, but some will be particularly emotional about the product and the results that they want to have. They will hit the buy button and that's about it.

After you have finalized the emotional close, you aren't done. It's important to introduce a logical close. The logical close includes sales arguments and rationale that transitions your prospect's way of thinking into tangible ideas. You go through the emotion and logic, and some people will buy at that point, but most won't. Most will continue reading into what they get immediately after purchasing, what they'll get out of the product, and when they can expect delivery if it's a physical product.

A popular section that works really well here is "This is what you'll receive immediately after purchase." Guarantees can also be included in this section because it's logical. Any kind of price breakdown fits well in this section also. If a product is $37, then you can actually justify the price as follows. "Give up a night out with the family for a life changing course that could give you more vacation time and a better life moving forward." Or, "For the price of a few lattes at Starbucks, you can be well on your way to earning five figures a month for the rest of your life." You can throw price comparisons and breakdowns in there because they're logical. After the logical section, allow them to purchase and click that Add to Cart button again.

The fear-based close is the last section. Lines like "There are only 500 copies available" or "There is only so much time, you only have until tonight at midnight!" or "I can't let too many people buy this product for fear of sabotaging the market." If it's a digital product, don't limit sales, limit time. An easy thing to do is include a live element, like a webinar, which is limited by nature, since as you can only have so many people tune in.

Video Sales Letter

One of the most effective sales tools in recent years is the video sales letter (VSL). A video sales letter is essentially a video version of the traditional long-form sales letter. The great news is that the skills you learn from writing sales letters and other copy apply to writing VSLs as well.

A video sales letter can contain any kind of video content you can create, even what you would typically see in TV commercials. However, for this book, we will focus on slideshow-style VSLs. These videos involve a Powerpoint-type presentation, narration, and optionally, a bit of music in the intro or close. The narrator can appear on camera, but that is usually not done.

If the product is something that can be demonstrated on screen, like software, you can include a short demo within the VSL. In the demo, just briefly show the product and mention some of the key features. For software you can make a separate demo or product tour video that goes into more detail; include a call to action at the end and put this video on its own web page. (Think of TV car commercials where they show the car and mention a couple of the top features, like the car gets 40 miles per gallon or seats seven adults, but they don't list every detail. Customers who want more details can look on the manufacturer's website or visit a dealer.)

How Long Should Your VSL Be?

When video sales letters first started appearing, some marketers went overboard and made VSLs that ran as long as an hour. Usually these videos do not have DVR-style controls that let the viewer fast forward through them. Just as bad, many of the pages these VSLs were on did not show the buy button until near the end of the video. So the viewer was forced to just sit there and let the entire video play or leave the site – even those people who were already ready to buy.

Don't make it hard for customers to give you money! To use the car analogy, if you walked into a dealership, told the salesperson which specific car on the lot you were ready to buy, and you had the cash on you to pay in full, what would they do? Insist that you take a test drive first or ask you to read some brochures? No! They would write up the sale and take your money as fast as possible before you could change your mind.

There is no magic length for a video sales letter, but for most offers, I suggest something in the 5-10 minute range. Offers that are more complicated or higher priced are worth a longer sales video than low-ticket offers. For example, a $1000 course with 30 modules should usually have a longer VSL than a $27 ebook. However, the VSL for the course doesn't need to go in depth about every module, or your sales video is going to be an hour long.

Upsell and downsell VSLs can be even shorter than that, since the customer has just made a purchase, and upsell/downsell offers usually don't need much explanation.

If you truly think your VSL needs to be 30 minutes or longer, I would strongly encourage you to do a webinar instead. People expect webinars to be 45-60 minutes or longer and won't get upset if one runs over an hour. However they are much less patient when it comes to VSLs. Part of that is that usually with a VSL, there is no easy way for viewers to tell how long the video will be. When the video starts playing, they don't know if it will be a minute long or an hour long.

Another reason why a webinar is better for longer presentations is simply that people have different expectations for a webinar. They often sign up days in advance, they put it on their calendar, they get reminder emails about it, they set aside an hour or longer, and they look forward to it. Some people register just hoping to catch the replay, though when a replay is ready, they know in advance to set aside an hour or so to watch it.

Think about how people will find your VSL. Maybe they just clicked on your ad. Maybe they did a search and your site came up. Or they got an email about your offer that linked to the VSL. Or they were already on your site poking around and found the VSL. In all of those cases, the visitor is not generally prepared to spend an hour watching your VSL. They might be ready to sign up for your webinar or watch a short VSL, though.

The Format of a Video Sales Letter

As I said above, a VSL is really just a video version of the traditional text-based sales letter, so most of the elements are the same.

A text sales letter needs to start with a great headline to grab people's attention. A VSL doesn't have a true headline, so you need to say something at the beginning to grab their attention and get them to watch.

A great way to do this is to ask them two or three Yes or No questions that would appeal to your ideal buyer. Preferably, an interested person's answer to the questions should be Yes. Basic psychology and persuasion teaches that getting your prospect to say Yes helps get them to take action when it comes to making a purchase or taking whatever action you want them to.

For example, say you're selling a weight loss system for men. Consider this opening:

Are you happy with your body? Do you like how you look with your shirt off?

Those questions are getting close to your ideal buyer, but they are phrased wrong, because the man who wants to lose weight is likely to answer No to both. Here is a better way to phrase them:

Are you tired of being fat and flabby? What would your life be like if you looked great with your shirt off?

See the difference there? With the second version, you'll get a resounding Yes to both questions, and you will also have your viewer imagining how great his life is going to be. He can probably already picture himself surrounded by models in bikinis, without you saying anything remotely like that.

If you already have a sales letter for your offer, you can usually come up with a good opener for your VSL by simply rephrasing the headline as a question.

People tend to use statements or claims as headlines, like this:

Amazing New Weight Loss System Will Have You Shedding Pounds in No Time!

We can rephrase that for the VSL something like this:

Would You Like to Shed Those Extra Pounds in No Time Flat?

I think you get the idea. For a real VSL I would probably add another question before that one, like this:

Are You Tired of Being Overweight? Would You Like to Shed Those Extra Pounds in No Time Flat?

See how the first question naturally flows into the second? In some cases you can chain together several questions like that which lead nicely into the meat of your VSL.

Another key difference between a text-based sales letter and a VSL is that the former is often dominated by bullet points. Sometimes a majority of the text is found in bulleted lists.

A VSL has more of a story structure than that. When you make your slides, you will probably have lots of bullets, but when you narrate the VSL out loud, it will sound like you're speaking in paragraphs, not reading a list of bullets.

A bullet on your VSL slide might be just a few words that people see while you narrate a whole paragraphs of two to four sentences.

Once you grab your prospect's attention, your VSL needs to tell them some type of story. A good format is the classic problem-solution-offer structure. The story is often how you (or whoever created the product or service) solved a problem or overcame some obstacles, and how that led to the creation of the product or service you're selling.

You've already stated the problem in the opening questions, so you can get right into the story of how you (or someone) had that problem and how you (or they) came up with the solution that you're now selling.

For the weight loss example, a classic story would be how you had been overweight for years, tried every diet, kept gaining back the weight, felt deprived, and so on. Then you stumbled on some special eating plan or combination of foods that let you lose the weight, keep it off, and it all fit well into your lifestyle. Maybe you went from couch potato to triathlete in a year.

Another angle for a story is from an expert's point of view, rather than a person who overcame the problem himself. In the weight loss niche, maybe a personal trainer or nutritionist or doctor came up with the solution, rather than the overweight person himself.

In that scenario, you could be the person who got help from the expert and is now motivated to help others, or you could be the expert (who maybe never was overweight himself) who came up with the solution to help your clients and has packaged it into a system that you're now selling.

Which of those angles should you go with? Whichever one is actually true!

Maybe what you're selling doesn't seem to be the solution to a problem. There is still usually a way you can find something to use this framework.

Let's say your product is a cookbook of your grandma's recipes. What problem does that solve? You could start your VSL talking about how we eat too much junk food, too much fast food, and too many microwaved meals, then talk about the benefits of wholesome, home-cooked meals and tell the story of how your family loved to gather around Grandma's table for whatever she was cooking. Now you've turned what could have been an ordinary cookbook into something special.

What Else Goes on Your VSL Page?

Typically right below a VSL is an order button or link. The call to action in the video can be something like "click the button below to get started" or "click the button below to order." Unless you're running a sale, there's no real need to mention the price in the VSL. Just display it on or near the order button. That way if you change the price, you won't have to edit the VSL (and you would definitely need to if you raise the price, because you don't want to say $27 in your video, then have people see that the price is actually $47).

You can put a traditional text headline above the VSL, or at least some text that encourages people to watch the video. It can be something like "New Video Reveals How to ..." or "Watch This Video to Learn About ..."

If you're going to be sending traffic from ads to the VSL, that headline should be consistent with your ad. It doesn't have to be word for word the same, but it should feel in sync with what your visitor just saw in your ad.

Some people like to put some copy below the VSL. This can be somewhat like a transcript of the VSL or even a long-form sales letter for the same product. The theory for doing this is that some visitors would rather read than watch a video or are in some situation where they can't watch a video (like at work), so the text version is for them.

Is that a good idea or not? The only way to know is to test it. In some cases adding the text version will increase sales for the reasons I've stated. In others it will actually distract people and decrease sales. A split test is the only way to tell whether it helps. Also, if your VSL is new and it doesn't convert well, you won't know if that's because of the text on the page or the video itself.

Start testing your VSL by just having the video, the order button, and the headline at the top. That way you'll know that whatever conversion numbers you see are due to the video or the headline. Once your VSL has decent conversion, you can consider split testing it against a page that also has the text copy below the video.

Who Should Narrate Your VSL?

You can narrate the video yourself or hire someone to do it for you. Many people don't like the sound of their own voices. This is mostly because your voice sounds different in your head than it does when recorded. Have you ever listened to a recording of your own voice and thought, "That doesn't sound like me"? We all have. The fact is, for some anatomical reasons, the voice we hear when we talk out loud is not the same as others hear. The recorded version is much closer to how the voice really sounds.

For most people, I would advise them to narrate their own VSL. If you're telling your own story, it sounds more authentic if you tell it yourself than if someone else tells it. This outweighs the fact that maybe you don't have a professional radio announcer voice. Most of us don't. Someone with a voice like that can do a great job of narrating, but it can come across as too slick or even phony.

There are other reasons to do your own narration. It will make you more confident about your ability to speak and present. That will come in handy if you do webinars or podcasts or are asked to speak at an event. When you get your own voice out there, your audience will start to recognize it, so when they see your VSL, it will match the voice they remember from the webinar or interview you did. You will always sound like you, but if you use a voiceover artist, what if you want more recording done and that person isn't available?

You can get a VSL recorded much faster by doing it yourself than waiting for a professional to do it. This makes it more practical to record multiple versions for testing and for targeting different audiences or angles. It also makes it much easier to make changes to your video if you can just record the new lines yourself in a few minutes.

There are two main reasons I can think of where it might make sense to outsource your narration. One is if you have a very thick accent that makes it too hard for others to understand what you're saying. The other is if you think an opposite-sex voice would be better to tell the story. For example, with that men's weight loss product, it would make more sense to have a male voice narrating it.

PART FIVE - EMAIL

.

Building An Email List

This fifth and final section of the book is all about list building and email marketing. List building is the practice of getting people to sign up for your email list, and email marketing is what you do after they subscribe.

Email marketing goes in waves. Every now and then, we read reports and blogs posts telling us that email is dead and building a solid email list is a waste of time.

I have to wholeheartedly disagree. It doesn't matter what niche or business you're in, your email list is one of your most valuable assets. In some cases, it's your ONLY asset!

After talking to clients over the years, there is lots of confusion over what's the best way to build a list, store a list, and market to a list.

Before we jump into squeeze pages, landing pages, email copywriting and all of that, we need to talk a little about what you need to start building a list so you have a good foundation.

NOTE: Having an email list isn't the same as blasting out an email to 100 contacts in Gmail! That's bad! There's a reason why software programs exist to help you manage your email list.

In this section, we're assuming nothing. If you've got a couple list building campaigns going, and they're working well – that's awesome! If not, that's ok too.

We're going to break list building down into its fundamental building blocks and build everything back up so that by the end of this section, if you follow along and go through all the tutorials, you'll have a fully functional campaign up and running.

With that being said, there are going to be things that we talk about here that you might already know. That's ok. Treat it as a refresher. Most likely, I might do things a little bit differently than you're used to, which is the point of learning!

Your #1 Priority As A Marketer

The idea behind list building is pretty simple. You give away something of value that'll help your prospects, and they give you their email address.

Then, as they grow to like and trust you, there is a certain number of prospects who will turn into paying customers, buying something that you have for sale or you're promoting as an affiliate.

Let's say you get 100 people who sign up to your list. 92 of those 100 people probably won't ever buy anything from you. Maybe they're not all that interested. Maybe they're broke. Maybe they don't like to put their credit card info into a web form.

There are lots of reasons why someone won't buy. Our job as email marketers isn't to concentrate on the non-buyers, though.

Our job is to find the buyers.

If 92 out of 100 won't ever buy… That means that 8 do!

Those 8 people will buy a lot, so it's important to keep mailing to them. That's why Scriptly does what it does – generate email autoresponders for you.

Behind Every Email Address…

Behind every single email address in your database is a human being. A real, live person reading your email, clicking your links, and either growing closer to you or further away.

It's easy to concentrate on the numbers and say that you have 34,000 people on your email address. What that means is that 34,000 people, at some point in time, gave your permission to send them email.

That invitation should not be abused.

When mailing your list, you should be genuinely interested in helping them with whatever they need help with – and the offers and content that you send them should further them in their mission.

If it doesn't, then you'll burn out your list pretty quick!

As we go through this section, we'll talk more in depth about list management but know that it's important to think of every email address on your list as a person.

Building an Email List

There are four things you need to build and profit from an email list, and each of these topics will be covered in this book, starting from the ground up.

1: Lead Magnets

The best way to think of your Lead Magnet is as a freebie or a loss-leader, designed to build your email list.

You create something of value that your prospects and customers will like, and in exchange for it, people give you their email address.

You have the ability to market to them in their inbox.

They have the ability to learn something from you!

It's a win-win.

There are lots of different lead magnets that you can create quickly. You just need to know where to start looking!

During this process, we're focusing 100% on creating Lead Magnets that drive conversions. Most people think that you start with a landing page or email marketing software.

That's not the case.

Setting up your landing page and your email autoresponder is relatively easy compared to penning a 10-page document worthy of giving away to your new prospects.
Plus, from a strategic standpoint, it's the most important part of your sales process!

Later in this book, we'll go through a few scenarios of creating and giving away lead magnets, including how you can use them to boost sales immediately after someone downloads one.

2: Landing Pages

Now, you're going to need a place to collect leads online.

This is where your traffic, your prospects, are going to sign up for your email list. It might be your blog, your landing page, products or services pages.

There needs to be a place online that people can sign up, whether that's your site or a piece of software that helps automate the process. Once the page is set up and you start collecting leads, we'll get into managing your list and email copy!

So, let's start with setting up a place to collect leads.

In this book, we'll be building landing pages that convert cold traffic to warm leads. We'll be looking at a variety of ways to build these landing pages.

Your landing page is where you convey the benefits of your lead magnet to your prospects. In other words, your landing page will answer the biggest question on your prospects minds, "Why should I sign up?"

A well-crafted landing page will convert anywhere between 30% and 60% of your total traffic from an ordinary browser to a qualified email lead. And once your visitor puts their email address in the opt-in box, your email marketing software will kick in!

3: Email Marketing Software (with Autoresponders)

Later we'll be talking about email marketing software, setting up your autoresponder messages, and we'll dig into affiliate training.

Your email marketing platform is the glue that holds this all together.

You can send broadcast messages. You can configure your autoresponder to send out an email every day promoting your products or services.

You can even arrange your buyer and affiliate lists separately, so you know exactly who you're mailing to!

Not to mention, your email marketing platform is what houses your email list and makes sure your email messages are CAN-SPAM compliant.

4: Traffic

The final step will be all about getting traffic to your landing pages. Facebook is easy to set up, instant, and cheap on a per-click basis. Plus, it's very scalable. If you can get 5 leads a day, you can get 500 leads a day once you prove out your campaign!

We can do all the work we want on the lead magnet, landing pages and the autoresponders. But if no one is coming to our landing page to opt in, we're not going to get any leads!

Get Ready!

Get ready for a roller coaster ride.

Soon you'll have your email marketing campaign set up. You'll have leads opting in to your email lists. And you'll be selling more products and services to a brand new channel of prospects!

Take this moment in. Relish it. Your business will be dramatically different in a few weeks, and you won't ever have to go back to looking for your next sale again!

Choosing The Right Platform

For the next few chapters, we're going to walk through all the aspects of email marketing, including setting up your list, building your landing pages, writing email copy and autoresponders, plus a ton of other stuff.

Ultimately, what we'll be doing is getting people to opt-in for your list!

Plus, we're going to talk a bit about traffic, so you can get started funneling traffic to your landing pages fast :0)

Now, a lot needs to happen between now and then, so, let's get started.

This is going to be an incredible section of the book, because as an Internet marketer your list IS your business.

It's your foundation.

You can always communicate with your list – your buyers and your prospects. You can mail affiliate products. You can do surveys. You can let people know about updates on your site or new product revisions.

Email is a very powerful medium when you understand it and actually use it correctly, which is what Scriptly helps you do!

Picking The Right Email Marketing Platform

Email marketing software is the glue that makes everything work. It's how you send emails to the folks on your list.

To put it simply, if you're collecting names and email addresses for the purpose of marketing, you've got to be CAN-SPAM compliant… Meaning every email needs to have an unsubscribe link, you need to include a physical address, and lots of other stuff.

There are LOTS of email software providers out there, all saying that they're the best. In actuality, they're all good. They get your emails where they need to go.

For our purposes, we want to make sure that:

- There is an autoresponder feature
- The software has the capability to grow with you
- Price-wise, it's reasonable based on the size of your business

So, here's a roundup of some of the best email marketing platforms out there, arranged by 'business complexity.'

Convertly.org

Convertly is my favorite email marketing software, mostly because my team created it for our clients… Out of all of the software solutions out there, there wasn't one that was easy to use (as in my mom could use it…) that I'd trust with my clients email automation. Not to mention, my clients need something that especially automated since all of the sales funnels we design and build are automated front to back.

… That also means that Convertly is awesome for you if you're just starting out too!

Besides doing broadcast emails, which means writing one email and sending it to the whole list, Convertly lets you set up a sequential series of emails that go out at a predetermined time based on when each person joined your list… And, you can import entire autoresponder sequences from our own, best selling Scriptly software!

So, if you want to build an automated sales funnel, email marketing is going to be right at the heart of it all!

When someone signs up for your newsletter, your free report, or for your download, they'll be put on an autoresponder that systematically sends out emails every day to them (or as often as you set them up…)

Deliverability is another factor. If you were to email your 200 clients out of Outlook or Gmail, chances are your server will shut you down for a little while. They do that to avoid spam. If you email those same clients from Convertly, your emails are almost guaranteed to get there!

OntraPort

If you have a list of 25,000 people or more, or you're going to be getting into heavy media buying, Ontraport is the way to go. They're by far my favorite of the more advanced CRM services out there, and they have a lot of additional features and capabilities that you'll need to grow your business.

Ontraport has been built from the ground up for serious Internet businesses. When we started using them, email marketing was why we switched over. We needed greater control over our data and more competitive email rates, and OAP gave that to us.

Now that we've built Convertly, we use Ontraport for everything else...

Things like:

- The shopping cart software (so you can sell stuff)
- A membership plugin for WordPress that integrates with said CRM system
- The ability to do direct mail, phone call followups, and task management
- Affiliate management software
- Plus, a ton of other stuff.

We use Ontraport to manage the financial side of the house basically.

InfusionSoft

Infusionsoft is awesome. It works very well, and is the standard when it comes to doing big business online...

Here's the thing though. I love how Infusionsoft works, but it's hard to use when you're starting out (for most people). To do one thing, like set up a product for sale that's delivered online through an email (like an ebook), you have to touch like six different screens.

With that being said, the power of the software is unparalleled when you know how to use it.

From a cost standpoint, starting up is pretty expensive as well. Not only do you have to pay the monthly charges, but you also have to pay a set-up fee that varies from time to time. I've seen it as high as $5,000, then a free setup, and now a $1500 setup that's waved if you're working with a Infusionsoft-certified consultant.

It's by no means the most expensive system, but it's quite pricey.

All of the things you'll love about OntraPort, can be found in Infusionsoft for half the price.

Depending on the plan you choose, Infusionsoft will be your:

- Customer Relationship Manager (CRM)
- Email marketing software
- Shopping cart provider, with quite a few merchant integrations
- Affiliate management software
- Plus a lot of other stuff...

I just know that I, as well as a lot of my clients, prefer to use OntraPort.

Up Next...

One thing you'll hear a lot when it comes to Internet marketing is the term 'landing pages' or 'squeeze pages'. They're really the cornerstone of your email marketing business.

Basically, landing pages are special kinds of web pages and websites that encourage a prospect to sign up for something. That something can be a free download of some kind, a free video, a free trial for a piece of software. Anything.

There are right ways and wrong ways of building squeeze pages, so we'll be talking about them later, including what software to use to make it easy for you.

Overall, having a landing page will take your conversion rate for your email sign up from 2% to 55% – meaning for every 100 people that see that page, 55 sign up!!

You can do a LOT with that kind of traffic on your email list!

Which email marketing platform are you using? Are you set up with Convertly? Do you have an email opt-in box on your website? Are you actively sending emails to your prospects and customers?

Lead Magnets

Growing a strong email list is all about turning clicks into leads, so that you can mail to them and drive revenue to your business.

There's a trick there though…

You have to give your visitors something of value that'll get them to enter their email address into your opt-in box!

Let's face it, the Internet is a big place and almost every topic known to man is beaten to death in various blogs, forum posts and news outlets. What makes your lead magnet so special that they can only get it from you?

If you're having trouble figuring out what would be a good lead magnet for your list, this chapter is for you.

Seven Types Of Lead Magnets

If you want to profit from your email list, you need to get the lead… There's no better way to do that than to start solving problems for your prospects and packaging the solution up into something that folks will opt-in for. Once you start getting leads, then you can start having Scriptly write your emails for you!

Here are seven major types of lead magnets. These aren't the only things you can use as lead magnets, but should give you some ideas to start with.

1. Report or Guide

The report is the standard lead magnet for good reason – it works! In fact, we've found that oftentimes a report or a guide will get cheaper, higher quality leads than a video ever will.

In the next chapter we'll talk more about how to create a report to use as a lead magnet.

2. Cheat Sheet or Process Map

I love process maps, because they cut through a lot of BS real quick. More to the point – your prospects will love process maps even more!

In a lot of instances, the sequence of events is what trips people up when they're trying to accomplish a certain task, be it setting up a website or editing a perfect black and white photo.

By outlining a complicated process and breaking it down into small, easily understandable chunks you're doing your folks an incredible service. They'll know that you:

- Have the process down to a science (increasing trust...)
- Are able to perform that process for them or teach them how to do it themselves

Both of those outcomes lead to more sales for you, in a very short amount of time!

3. Software

Software was what I was meant to do with my life, and I'm just now finding that out.

One of our software applications is TimeSlots, a sales call scheduling software. It has a 14-day free trial. I don't need to tell you how awesome that is for getting us leads! You can see it at timeslots.org.

The beauty of software is that its core function is to solve a problem for users, instantly. Plus, there's an immediate gratification element to it that can't be matched.

The best way to turn your software into a lead magnet is to have a Free Trial set up. They get full access to all of the features of your software, and after 7 days or 14 days they need to join to keep using it.

4. Checklists

Much like process maps, checklists are awesome tools for describing a set of actions that someone needs to take to accomplish a task correctly, without actually giving them the tools and the training to do it…

The 2X checklist is what we gave away on some of our live webinars.

(After all, we do want to convert them to a sale at some point, right?)

With a well thought out checklist, you can demonstrate that you know the material inside and out, and also point out things that your prospect might be missing!

This is great for getting them to raise their hand and say that they need your help!

5. Videos

One of the ways that a lot of marketers try to get leads is to give access to a free video. From experience, I can tell you that sometimes it works…   And sometimes it doesn't.

If you're demonstrating something that's highly visual, like training a dog, swinging a golf club, adjusting a camera for the best portrait, or building something out of 2×4's, then video is a good medium to share that content.

If you're doing something that's NOT visual, like talking about marketing strategy, explaining the big benefit of life coaching, or teaching someone how to ward away panic attacks – a video lead magnet is a bad way to go.

The point of video is to move them along in the sales process, and it's almost impossible to do if the video isn't engaging. You're far better served to choose some kind of PDF download that you can give away.

6. Tutorials

 I'm a big fan of point and click tutorials for teaching– and they make excellent lead magnets.

In fact, I can't tell you how many people have emailed me saying the printed them out and rely on them every time they need to set up a new campaign or a new website.

As further evidence of this, one of the biggest tutorial sites online is Envato Network's TutsPlus. For years, they've put together incredible tutorial sites, and now they've got so much content that they've put a big ecourse kind of wrapper around it, making it a HUGE challenger in the digital course space!

7. Quiz or Survey

And finally, quizzes and surveys.

What's funny is that quizzes and surveys have been around forever, and marketers are just now touting them as the 'best way to engage users' because you can get feedback from your readers a bit differently.

Years ago, we called this list segmentation… When someone fills out a survey and selects (A) as their choice, they get put into one autoresponder. If they select (B), they get put in another autoresponder.

That's the crux though… When you use a survey as a lead magnet, your lead conversion will most likely drop… But your engagement will be a lot higher, meaning you'll have better quality leads!

It's worth testing. I've seen campaigns that use surveys so effectively that it doubles opt-in rates. I've also seen campaigns where conversions were below 10% (which is dismal!) It's all in how you set them up!

(We've actually used surveys so often (and so effectively) that we built out own survey tool, **Askly.org**, to handle them for us. It does rules based segmentation, URL forwarding based on answers, and all sorts of other cool stuff!)

After You Get The Lead…

After you get the lead, what do you do? Do you sell them something? Do you give them a bunch of free content and build a relationship with them?

The best answer – both!

Inside Scriptly, we have dozens of email templates that'll move prospects from just getting to know you to buying your stuff as soon as you send out an email. It's all copy and paste.

Go here to watch the video:

http://scriptly.org/video

Creating A Lead Magnet

Growing a strong email list is all about turning clicks into leads, so that you can mail to them and drive revenue into your business.

There's a trick there though…

You have to give your visitors something of value that'll get them to fill their email address into your opt-in box!

Let's face it, the Internet is a big place and almost every topic known to man is beaten to death in various blogs, forum posts, and news outlets. What makes your lead magnet so special that they can only get it from you?

That's what we're going to talk about in this chapter. And the first thing we need to cover is what constitutes a good lead magnet.

Then, of course, we're going to talk about how to create one!

The Most Important Part of Your Lead Magnet

The first thing we need to get out in the open is that most lead magnets suck. The reason you don't get more than 15% conversions on landing pages doesn't have anything to do with the page itself…

It's your lead magnet!

The key is to be specific – to let a prospect know exactly what they're downloading. What does a super specific lead magnet title let you do on the thank you page?!

Add an upsell!

That's right… If someone just downloaded a report titled, "7 Secret Persuasion Tricks To Increase Webinar Conversion," what do you think they're interested in?

Webinars!!

Which means you can sell webinar courses, done for you services, coaching, and anything in between.

Welcome to the magic of creating sales funnels.

Now, let's get back to lead magnets. There are seven different types of lead magnets that we use, with a very strong preference to #1 and #5…

Creating Your First Lead Magnet

The first type of lead magnet that we're going to use for your campaign is a report or a guide.

Special reports or guides get great opt-ins, they're easy to create, and you've already got all of the software that you need to get one set up on your computer.

Plus, we've found that oftentimes a report or a guide will get cheaper, higher quality leads than a video ever will.

There are some things to take note of when it comes to creating a report to give away, including:

- You MUST, MUST, MUST deliver value.
- Your reader should have the ability to DO something contained in the report that will give them gratification of some kind.
- There should be at least a little bit of bonding that takes place in the report, so your new lead gets to learn a little more about you!
- A good length for a free report is 8 to 12 pages, normal spacing and typefaces. (People don't value a 50 or 100-page free report nearly as much as you might think.)
- Most important of all - it needs to focus on ONE specific, clearly identified problem!
- And… Make sure it contains some kind of call to action at the end of it!

With reports, the more clearly you state the benefit, the better your conversions and lead costs will be from paid traffic.

Let's get into your step-by-step action plan:

1. Figure Out What Your Lead Magnet Will Be About

The first thing you need to think about is what your lead magnet will be about. (See the next chapter for a whole slew of ideas)

There's a fair bit of strategy that comes into play here, because you want your lead magnet to stand out among all of the other ones out there

And you want to use your lead magnet as a way to position you and your products correctly, since you're going to be selling to these leads through email!

A friend of mine, Ryan Deiss, says that lead magnets should be 'splinters' of what you're selling. In other words, they should be small, little sections of the bigger product.

For example:

- If you have a course on real estate investing, your lead magnet might be a report on "3 Ways To Find Cheap Investment Opportunities Using Free Tools."
- If you have a coaching offer on webinar marketing, you could have a lead magnet titled, "7 High Intensity Closing Strategies That'll Increase Webinar Conversions By 120 Percent."
- If you've got a brick and mortar shop - a car dealership - your report might be "5 Things To Look For That'll Maximize Your Car's Resale Value."

In each of those examples, the lead magnet is a small, microscopic part of the larger, overall picture!

A side benefit is, since you're just giving away a piece or a splinter of a bigger picture, your lead magnet will be ultra-focused and easily understood by cold traffic. That means your conversions will be through the roof.

Anyone can write a report titled "7 Ways To Double Your Revenue," or "8 Conversion Hacks For Your Website." Take 5 minutes and cruise around online and you'll be surprised how many similar titles you'll find.

The key is to be specific – to let a prospect know exactly what they're downloading – and make sure that the material is unique enough that the only way for them to consume it is to actually go through the lead magnet!

Because let's face it… If your lead doesn't at least look at your stuff, they sure won't be on your list for very long! How many times have you downloaded something and never looked at it?

So, rather than totally start from scratch, let's just see if we can give the first title, "7 Ways To Double Your Revenue," a makeover...

- 7 Secret Persuasion Tricks To Increase Webinar Conversion
- 7 WordPress Plugins That Increase Visitor Engagement (Without Them Even Realizing It!)
- 7 Passive Ad Networks That'll Increase Website Revenue In The Next 15 Minutes
- 7 Email Templates To Re-Engage The Email Subscribers Who Have Already Written You Off

See how that works?

Be specific. Deliver value. Get the lead.

2. Open Up Your Editor

Now that you've decided on what your lead magnet will be about, it's time to open up your word processor. Depending on your computer and operating system, there are four different programs that you can choose from:

- Microsoft Word
- Apple Pages
- Google Docs
- OpenOffice

It doesn't matter to me which one you use. I'm a Mac guy and prefer Pages, but it's completely up to you. From a functionality standpoint, they each do the same thing.

In terms of style and logistics, just use the default settings for margins and spacing. Don't worry about making the font bigger or changing the style.

Some notes:

- Include an intro section. Talk about what's going to be in the report, introduce yourself to your new reader, and make sure to talk about why what they're about to read matters.
- Include subheadings. Break up longer sections of your lead magnet into sections and give them sub-headlines. This encourages consumption.
- Write like you would to a friend. Lead magnets serve three purposes - to educate, to bond your new visitor to you, and to sell. Don't write them like you would a research paper or a corporate memo...

3. Write 8-12 Pages

We've found that your lead magnet reports should be between 8 to 12 pages long. That might sound like a lot, but it goes by fast!

In fact, here's a little breakdown that you can use as a model for yourself:

- Introduction: 1 Page
- About You: 1 Page
- Report Core: 5 Pages (this is the meat of your report)
- Summary: 1 Page
- Call To Action: 1 Page

And really, the title of your lead magnet is going to give you everything you need to beef up that report core section.

If you're writing a report titled, "7 High Intensity Closing Strategies That'll Increase Webinar Conversions By 120 Percent," simply devote a page to each of those seven strategies and you're golden!

Again, make sure to include sub-headlines to break up each section.

4. Include Calls to Action

At the end of your report, you'll want to include a call to action to your sales video, webinar signup page, affiliate link, or whatever you're promoting.

You want to give your reader the opportunity to read the report and then click through to continue deeper into your sales funnel.

Usually, the very last section in our reports is a "What's Next?" or "Next Steps" section.

In that section, I invite a reader to continue on the journey by signing up for a webinar, filling out a strategy session form, or watching a video. In each of those examples, they continue deeper on the path.

The person who opts in, downloads your report, then reads through the entire thing and clicks through a link is an extremely hot lead.

They liked you. They liked what you had to say. And they're willing to take the next step with you – which means you're about to generate some revenue!

These are your buyers, which we talked about before.

5. Add Images

After you include your call to action, it's time to pretty up your report a little bit.

I'm not huge on adding images to every page of a report, but I do try to make my stuff at least a little bit graphically appealing. You can go off the deep end fast, by hiring an editor and having them mock up a design for the whole report.

164

Typically, what I'll do is look for Creative Commons or royalty-free images that correspond to the sections of my report, and drop them in.

One thing you do want to make sure to include is a picture of yourself! Your readers want to learn more about you, and there's no better way of fostering a bond than including an image of yourself.

6. Export as a PDF

In Step 2, we listed several different word processors you can use to write your report. Each of them has the functionality of exporting your document as a PDF.

PDFs are the standard when it comes to reports. They lock the editor so that a reader can only read what you wrote, and Adobe Reader (the program that opens up PDFs) is on almost every computer known to man.

Plus, your more technologically proficient readers will be able to put their PDF on their Kindle, iPad, or Android tablet, and consume your content from there.

Not to mention, with Amazon Kindle and iBooks getting so popular, ebooks and digital files have more value associated with them. That's a good thing in the mind of your prospect!

7: Upload Your PDF to Share Online

The last step is to upload your PDF online somewhere, so you can share it by posting a link.

There are a lot of ways to do this… You can upload your PDF to Dropbox.com and share it with a public link. You can upload it to Google Drive and give it a public link. You can upload it to your server with an FTP program such as FileZilla.

Or, my favorite, you upload your document as a media file to your WordPress website and get your link from there:

1. Log into your WordPress administrator panel.
2. Click on Media on the menu in the left column.
3. Click the Add New button at the top.
4. Drag your PDF document as directed on the page, or click the Select Files button, then choose the PDF file.
5. Once the PDF file is uploaded, click on the icon for it that WordPress just added to the page.
6. Look for the URL field on the upper right of the page. Copy the entire contents of this field. This link is what you give to people so they can download your PDF.

Creating Lead Magnets with Curately

Another way to create a lead magnet is by using one of our software tools, Curately. You've probably heard of content curation, which is the practice of gathering content from around the web and presenting bits of it to your audience with proper attribution and links back to the original source.

That last part is important. It's the difference between the routine, legitimate practice of content curation and copyright infringement. You can't just to to another site, copy entire posts or articles, and slap it on your site.

You can do curation manually. A common way of doing this is to find a really good article or post on another site, write a summary of it in a couple of sentences, then put that summary on your site with a link to the original. This is a win/win/win scenario. It's a win for the original site because it gets a link from you and the social proof of you citing it as a good source of content. It's a win for your readers because they find good content that they probably haven't seen before. And it's a win for you, because you get good content on your site without creating the whole piece, you look good (and selfless) to your readers for sharing it with them, and you look good to the original site by citing them.

What Curately does is dramatically speed up this process. It lets you easily search for content you might want to curate, pick the items you want to use, and generate a post from them on your blog that you can then make final edits to.

Curately is NOT a "scraper" or automated blogging tool. There has been a lot of software that just went out and copied a bunch of content from around the web, just to create a bunch of pages on a site, usually so the new site owner could slap ads on those pages. This was not about quality or serving the readers. It was about trying to make a fast buck, and there was usually no filtering or quality check to find great content, just to grab a lot of content to fill a bunch of pages.

That's not curation- it's copying, and it can get you in lots of trouble. The owners of the sites you copy from can come after you, you can look bad to your readers for having a bunch of content that may not be the best, and you can possibly lose your advertising accounts by putting ads on what the company decides are low-quality sites.

Curately does almost the exact opposite of what those content copying programs do. It assists you in finding good content and in putting together snippets of it, but it also allows you the final decision of which pieces of content to curate and how to arrange them. It does what you would do manually, but much faster. It takes most of the grunt work out of curation, but there is some thought required on your part. :) It's not for the lazy, fast-buck artists who don't care about what ends up on their sites.

Besides building curated posts for you, Curately can also create PDFs, which you can then use as lead magnets.

To learn more about Curately, go watch the video at **curately.org/video**.

What's Next?

Now, you have everything you need to start writing your first lead magnet…

- Figure out what you're going to write about.
- Give it a title.
- Open up your favorite word processor and start writing.
- Export it as a PDF, so your readers can download and read it.
- Upload it online and save your link to share!

That link – the one that you have for your PDF – is what we're going to use when we set up our email autoresponder. That link will go in the very first autoresponder message that we send out, after someone opts in.

We've got some other stuff that we need to get through before we get there though, so be patient :0)

Landing Pages That Convert

In this chapter, we're going to talk about something that you're going to want to really understand when it comes to email marketing and setting up an automated sales system.

Collecting leads in the sidebar of your website or at the bottom of your post is effective, but it's going to be hard to build a huge list that way unless you have hundreds of thousands of visitors a month.

Let me put it this way.

When you put your opt-in box in your sidebar, it's easy to miss. A reader will check out your content and unless they really want to hear from you again, just leave. If your content is stellar, then they might sign up if you give them an incentive.

That means that your conversion rates are going to be really low! So let's start with that.

Understanding Conversion Rates

Conversion rates are pretty easy to get through. Very simply, it's the number of people who SEE your opt-in form compared the the number of people who fill it out.

So, if 100 people see your opt-in box and 50 fill it out, your conversion rate is 50%.

If 100 people see your opt-in box and 5 fill it out, your conversion rate is 5%.

Well, typically when you put your opt-in box in the sidebar, you'll get less than a 1% conversion rate; meaning that fewer than 1 person out of 100 wants to hear from you again!

Does Ugly Still Work?

Now, over the years, landing pages have gotten a tad bit more sophisticated because of the user experience that certain ad networks force on us. For the most part though, they're pretty straightforward.

Sure, best practices change from time to time. Do we put up ugly pages with a big headline? Do we need graphical pages that look pretty? Does a double-click opt-in work better than a straight up form?

In the rest of this section, I'll share some of our best practices for generating leads and the nuts and bolts of setting up landing pages. For the time being though, we're going to take baby steps. We're going to start our conversation talking about the psychology and the tools you'll need to start getting leads!

The first thing we need to get through is where your landing page will be located online. Typically when you put your opt-in box in the sidebar, you'll get less than a 1% conversion rate; meaning that fewer than 1 person out of 100 wants to hear from you again! (Also, many people just ignore sidebars because that's where so many sites put ads.)

Self-Hosted vs. App-Hosted

There are two different ways to set up a landing page – on your own domain with your own web hosting (AK self-hosted). Or with a service that takes care of that for you (AKA app-hosted).

There are advantages and disadvantages to each, and you'll have to decide for yourself which you're more comfortable with. After all, the leads that you get will be going into your own email marketing software, so those are yours for good.

First, let's talk about self-hosted landing pages, or setting up and maintaining your own website.

To create and host your own website, you absolutely need two things:

- A domain name
- Website hosting

The easiest and fastest way to get set up is to go through HostGator. Choose the domain that you want for your website, pick a hosting package, and then install WordPress.

At the end of the day, the software industry understands that setting up and maintaining a website is difficult (albeit a very valuable skill if you take the time to learn it!).

So, they've created software that makes setting up landing pages and sales pages much easier. I'll discuss some of these software options later in this chapter.

With landing pages, there are really very few places to go if you don't enter your email address. That's the idea. If the person wants the information on the other side, they have to give up an email address!

At the end of the day, there is no one best choice. Whether you build your own landing pages or rely on a service that you pay monthly for is up to you. There are some points to consider though.

Self Hosted Landing Pages:

- Having everything set up on your own website, with your own web server is the absolute safest option in terms of data backups and having complete control over your data.
- You can do things on your own website that will increase conversion of your pages, that app-hosted pages might not allow.
- It'll take some time to get set up, as learning to build, maintain and manipulate WordPress and WordPress pages takes some time.

App Hosted Landing Pages:

- It's much faster to deploy your first landing page, using a piece of software like Scriptly.
- You get proven templates and designs right off the bat, so you spend less time testing.

Landing Page Psychology

Landing pages (or squeeze pages as they're called) do something very simple – they collect email addresses from people who may or may not be willing to spend money with you in the future.

They give you their email address with the express consent that you can contact them in the future through email.

You give them some kind of something that incentivizes the prospect to sign up. That something is lead magnets we discussed in previous chapters.

It goes a little deeper though. If you read the book "Influence: The Psychology of Persuasion" by Dr. Robert Cialdini, you start to see something else at work.

That something is reciprocity.

Basically, the Law of Reciprocity says that if you do something for someone else, they are morally committed to doing something for you. They feel like they have to.

So, by giving you a free download, you are committing them to read a report, watch a video, or otherwise spend money with you.

That, my friends, is the biggest key behind why squeeze pages work. Sure, you have the person's name and email address. But the true power lies in the Law of Reciprocity.

Landing Page Setup

Now, it's time to create a landing page!

There are quite a few ways of doing it because there are so many marketers using WordPress, but I'll keep this simple.

If you want one piece of software that you can use for all of your landing pages, you can sign up for one of the services like Scriptly.

If you'd rather work with WordPress, there are several themes and plugins which have features designed for building landing pages. Since the WordPress marketplace is constantly changing, we won't discuss specific themes and plugins in this book.

You can of course code up your own if you know HTML and have Photoshop! I'm sure not that ambitious though.

So, let's look at Scriptly.

Scriptly

Scriptly is our copywriting software. It has a built-in landing page creator. It can also write your email sequences, sales webinars, video sales letters, and more.

Scriptly also has a landing page builder built into it, so you can use it to create your opt-in pages, confirmation pages, call signup pages, webinar pages, sales pages, and almost any other type of web page you might want to build.

Check it out at **scriptly.org.**

Some Stuff You Need To Know

Not many people do email list management justice. Just because someone opted into your newsletter doesn't mean that they want to hear from you! Here are a few things you'll need to pay attention to make sure your emails get delivered, make you money, and keep you out of the doghouse.

Double opt-in – make sure that people click a verification link in their email to actually opt in to your list. This is BIG when it comes to spam complaints.

Non active subscribers – In our email marketing software we have it set up so that after 120 days of not taking action, subscribers are automatically deleted off of our lists. We do this for two reasons: it keeps our costs down and only people who care about our content actually read our stuff!

Relevant subject lines – Make sure the subject line of the email is relevant to what's in the email (and stay away from 'Notification of Payment Received' or other that imply they have made a sale or earned a commission or other deceptive subject lines). People get upset if your subject line is misleading.

Advertisement announcement – Include somewhere in the email, preferably the extreme bottom, that the email message is an advertisement, and for the reader to assume that you are somehow making money from anything that they do.

Email frequency – Take note of how often you email, and what your responses are from your list. Some lists mail daily. Others a few times a week. We've found that it's best to take breaks, and then follow that up with a 3 or 4 day sequence of emails.

Up Next

Now that you're email list is off and running, and you'll be setting up a landing page in the next few days, it's time to talk about list management.

There are best practices when it comes to your list that you're going to want to follow!

I can't say that we send billions of emails a year or anything like that, but we've tested out a lot of different things including bonding messages, pitches, webinars, and so on.

You've Got A Lead. Now What?

Getting leads to sign up for your email list is pretty straightforward, isn't it?

We've already talked about how to create a lead magnet. We do up a landing page and set up your email marketing platform. Where do they go after that though?

What do your prospects do **immediately after they sign up on your list**?

Well, my friends. Immediately after your folks sign up on your list, you should be making them an offer.

Your brand new lead is **never more engaged with you than they are immediately after downloading your lead magnet**.

NEVER.

If you miss the opportunity to pitch them something, it's going to be the last time that you'll be seeing a lot of these folks.

Think about this. Open rates for the first week after someone signs up for your list are typically 40% to 55% – give or take depending on the market or niche.

That means, roughly HALF of your new leads sign up for your lead magnet and never open any more emails from you.

So, if you're paying for traffic, you can legitimately wipe 5 out of every 10 leads away. You got their email address, but you won't be getting anything else.

Some of them might unsubscribe. Some might report you as spam. The rest will be disengaged.

The remaining half, the **engaged, active part of your new list**… They'll open your emails, click your links, and they'll buy eventually; but that doesn't do anything for the ad budget that you just spent to get them!

So in this chapter, what I want to talk about is making an offer on the thank you page of your list building campaign. (NOTE: I call these 'Thank You Funnels' for future reference!)

Here's how to do it:

Your thank you page is the second-most important page on your site (following your landing page, of course). It's the page people are taken to after they opt in, which usually says something like "Thank you for subscribing."

I'm going to show you how to make an offer on your thank you page that moves a new prospect over into being a fully-fledged buyer pretty quickly.

That way, you can turn that new revenue back into ad spend so you can keep scaling your campaign.

This is also important, because once someone has made a purchase from you, even if it's only $1, they are much more likely to buy from you again.

And just so you know, this is preferably done in video, but it can be accomplished in a text-based page too.

Step 1: Thank Your Prospect

The first thing you want to do is thank your new prospect for taking the time to download your lead magnet.

This is easy enough to do with a headline or the opening of the video being:

Thank you so much for downloading (insert lead magnet title here).

You can even do it in a news bar across the top of the page.

Just make sure there is a confirmation on the page or in the video somewhere.

Step 2: Confirm Arrival Times

Next, you want to tell your prospect what to expect by way of arrival.

Are they downloading the lead magnet from the page they're on? Are they going to be receiving it in their email? What I generally do is send it as a link through email, and I tell them when to expect it:

Your download link will be in your inbox in 5 to 10 minutes!

Two good reasons to deliver your lead magnet link via email: it forces people to give you a valid email address if they want to receive your lead magnet, and it gets them used to opening your emails and clicking links in them.

Most autoresponders will send your first email instantly, but sometimes it'll take a few minutes to get to your prospect. A lot of that depends on network congestion, times of the day, etc.

Ideally, you want your prospect to watch your video or read your entire thank you page before they go check their email though. Telling them that it'll be ready in a few minutes serves two purposes – it keeps them there for a few minutes and it gives your email platform a chance to send that first email.

Step 3: Position And Pivot

This step, Position And Pivot is the most important when it comes to your Thank You Funnel succeeding.

When you put yourself in your prospects shoes, they've just downloaded a report that they hope will help them solve a problem or do something better. They haven't seen it yet though.

So, it's important to position the video that they're watching as a way of achieving their desired result faster!

You can do this by using simple language like:

> *Now that you've downloaded the 100 Most-Opened Subject Lines Report, you've got a proven set of plug and play phrases that'll get you better open rates in your emails...*
> *When you watch this video until the end, you'll also be able to access the email autoresponder sequences that'll get your list buying your products and services!*

Another way of doing this is by posing a question:

> *The first question I get asked by people who download the Lines Report is how to write the body of the email copy. What to put where.*
>
> *And when you watch this video until the end, you'll know what the best way of writing copy is. In fact, by the time you finish this video, you'll know all about a piece of software that'll write your email autoresponders for you!*

The pitch, of course, would be Scriptly's Autoresponder Engine, but we're not there yet…

First, we need to deliver some content.

Step 4: Deliver Content & Value

Before we can make the pitch, we have to deliver some content and value. This is where your thank you video turns into a full-on sales pitch.

The normal story arc in a sales pitch is this:

- Establish that there is a problem
- Introduce yourself (and how you were faced with that problem)
- Relate the problem to yourself in story form.
- Describe your journey in solving the problem for yourself
- Introduce the product or service that contains the solution (with full-on features and benefits)

Now, I realize that your product or service might not lend itself to this sort of a sales scenario. If you're selling software, you might want to put a demo video here. If you're selling a video course or a membership, it might be beneficial to dig right into the benefits of what you're selling.

It'll take some creativity and testing to pull this off, but it'll be well worth your time. We can take a look at doing it for you at **DoneForYou.com** too.

Step 5: Make The Pitch

Now that we've positioned our video and pivoted away from the lead magnet, it's time to ask for the sale.

Ideally, pricing for this thank you page offer is below $50, and serves as the first product that your prospects can buy from you. If they go through the order process, they'll they hit a few one-click upsells ranging from $50 to $300.

Depending on your market, products below $10 work very well for the first offer. These markets include business, marketing, survival, dating, and health.

In some markets though, you want to be closer to the $50 range. Examples for the higher-tier pricing include investment information and photography.

In the photography market, your buyers are used to spending $1000 for a camera, $200 for a tripod, $40 for text book style education. So, the higher-end pricing is justified.

In other markets where there is information everywhere, in every form (like business), you'll need to stay below $10 for your front end sale.

At the end of the day, you want to turn your leads into revenue as quickly as possible, and this thank you funnel does that. It turns your most engaged prospects into customers, and marches them through an upsell funnel without betraying them or shoving products down their throat.

That way, you can take your newly generated revenue and drive more traffic with it!

Inside Scriptly, there are autoresponder sequences that'll help automate the backend of this process for you as well, with the Product Sales Sequence and the Ascension Sequence being the ones you'll use :0)

The Product Sales Sequence is the set of emails that you send out following the download link. And the Ascension Sequence are the emails that you queue up for anyone who buys your front end product!

Writing Clickable Email Copy

Writing email copy is a pain... I'm not going to lie.

Not only do you have to know exactly what you want your prospects to do ahead of time, but you also need to chain together enough emails that you can effectively promote your product or offer days in advance!

Sure you can sit down at your desk every single day and write one email, but stuff pops up. You'll be interrupted and fires will need to be put out... Emails are one of easiest things to push off!

When you hear the terms sales copy or email copy, it's just the way that you write sales messages or email messages that incite some type of action from your prospect :0)

That action can be a click, a sale, or watching a video. That's how you sell stuff! If no one clicks, buys, or watches, then your copy is the first place you have to start troubleshooting!

There is an art to writing emails that people open, read, and ultimately click through, and that's what this article is about.

Before we get to writing email though, we need to take a step back and figure out what exactly we're trying to get our list to do – in micro-steps.

Our Goal In Writing Email Copy

Email copy is an interesting animal, in and of itself.

You see, your emails don't typically do the selling for you. Sure, you can link right to an order form and you'll get a few sales, but the much more typical way of using email to get buyers is to link to a sales page, like this:

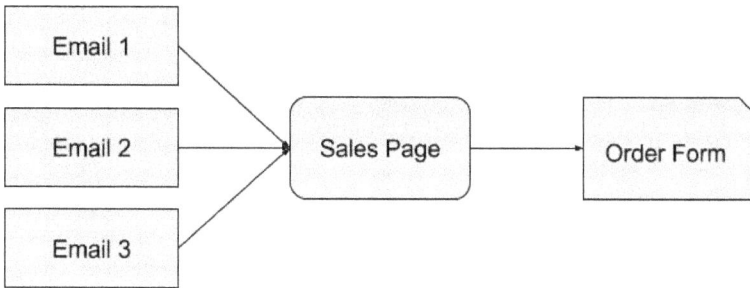

```
┌─────────────┐
│   Email 1   │ ╲
└─────────────┘   ╲
                    ╲
┌─────────────┐      ╭──────────────╮        ┌──────────────┐
│   Email 2   │ ────→│  Sales Page  │───────→│  Order Form  │
└─────────────┘      ╰──────────────╯        └──────────────┘
                    ╱
┌─────────────┐   ╱
│   Email 3   │ ╱
└─────────────┘
```

The flow looks simple enough…

Email your prospect a link to your sales page, they click through to the order form and buy!

Here's the challenge though…

Not everyone on your will open your email, let alone click the link to the sales page. (Some of them won't even receive your message, for various reasons.)

Which means there are a specific set of micro-actions associated with your email, which'll make the whole thing work.

(Note: the sooner you understand this idea of 'micro-actions,' the quicker you'll be able to turn your campaigns around! It took me a long time to figure this out.)

For every person who receives your email, they all must do three things before they hit your sales page:

- They have to open your email
- They must at least start to read your body copy

- They need to click a link in your email

All of that has to happen BEFORE they see your sales page!

So, when you're breaking down the results you get from your email marketing campaign, take a step back and think about the metrics associated with those micro-actions!

How many people opened the email?

How many people clicked the link to the sales page?

Those are your defining metrics when it comes to email copy...

Here's the thing though... The goal of your email isn't to sell the product. The goal is to get the click. Let the sales page sell the product!

Now, let's talk about what you can do to get the best results possible from your email, starting with the idea of 'preframing.'

Preframing Correctly

Preframing is an NLP technique used by copywriters to get a prospect or user to take action. The dictionary definition is "setting in advance the boundary conditions of an experience or event, often then changing the outcome."

You don't need to get crazy into NLP or anything to understand how to use it though!

Basically, successfully preframing someone is all about setting them up to take action on the next page, after they click the link in your email.

I'm actually running a paid traffic campaign in the photography niche right now where we're collecting email addresses. Right after they sign up, they get an email from me with some email copy and a link to a sales page.

Rather than say, "Check out this photography course. It's got lots of training on picking the right camera, using Photoshop, and taking expert pictures..."

My email copy says, "Imagine using X technique to sharpen your clients photos," or "Y strategy really has served as inspiration for a lot of the landscape photos that I've been taking..."

The conditions being: X technique, Y strategy

The experience or event being: their education after purchasing the product!

Make sense?

Preframing is the biggest difference between marketers who make HUGE money and marketers who don't.

You can use it everywhere, including:

- Email messages you send out in your autoresponder
- Landing pages that come before the actual product, like download pages, reviews, and advertorials
- Sales copy you write, either as video sales letters or long form sales messages
- Webinars that you do with your audience, talking about the benefits of a product before the product is revealed.

Unfortunately, it's not something that you just get. It takes practice (or using a tool like Scriptly).

Now that that's out of the way, let's talk about your email copy!

Writing Solid Email Copy

Writing good, clickable email copy follows a specific formula that can be mastered, as long as you start with an end result in mind.

Your entire email (and the whole autoresponder series that you're writing to promote a product) needs to accomplish one thing...

To get at least one click to the sales page.

You want as many people on your list as possible to click through, and sometimes that takes a few emails to do!

Step 1: Start With The End In Mind

What do you want your email list to do?

Do you want them to read a blog post? Or click through to a sales page? Or sign up for a brand new lead magnet? Or maybe, register for a free workshop that you have coming up.

It's rare that you'll be sending your list an email without some specific action in mind...

When you send an email, you're:

- Trying to build a relationship with them
- Wanting to re-engage with them
- Selling them something

181

- Getting them to sign up for something

That's why the Scriptly Autoresponder Templates are designed the way they are… To get some sort of action from your email list!

Once you figure out what specific action you want your email list to take, it's time to create a campaign around that action.

Step 2: Write a Strong Subject Line

The subject line is the first thing that your prospect sees in their inbox, and is the biggest factor in whether or not they'll read your email or not.

There are LOTS of different types of subject lines, including:

- The "Ask A Question" subject line
- The "How To" subject line
- The "Scarcity" subject line
- The "Brand New" subject line
- The "Numbers" subject line
- The "Curiosity Gap" subject line
- The "Shock And Awe" subject line
- The "Named" subject line

At the end of the day, you need to appeal to the prospect and make them interested or curious enough to open the email.

The FTC says that you have to adequately describe what is in the email, although that's pretty vague. Something as simple as 'New Stuff' does technically describe what's in the email.

Elements of a great subject line include:

- Curiosity – Make them so curious that they have to open the email to find out the rest of the story. (ie. Bad News)
- Contradiction – Contradict something that is normally held to be true (i.e. SEO is dead!)
- Specificity – Specifics help make the subject line more real (i.e. THIS gets 62% more opt-ins!)
- Personal Touch – Make them feel like the email is from a friend… not from a business marketing to them. (i.e. Hey!)
- Instant Usability – Make them feel there is something for them they can instantly use to get a desired result (i.e. PDF Download Inside!)

I tend to be along the 'Instant Usability' spectrum, but that's just me.

Did you think this was going to be complicated? It really isn't!

Nothing really beats good split testing. In most email marketing platforms, you can split test subject lines so you can really nail down which ones get opened and which ones don't.

The more people that open the email and read it, the more clicks you'll get. The more clicks, the more income!

Step 3: The Email Body

Writing email copy is pretty easy, especially when you've got a great subject line.

The most obvious thing is to talk more about the subject of the email, explaining it, and fulfilling on the promise of what will happen when someone opens to email up.

The next thing you want them to do is to take action.

You want them to click something in your email. That's the whole reason for sending an email to them in the first place right?

In almost every email, you want your prospect to take an action, which is usually clicking on a link.

Keep in mind, there's a person reading this email. Too often, when an email marketer knows that there are 70,000 prospects reading their emails, they forget to write for one person. They think that if they blast out an image or a banner, they'll get results.

They don't.

The key to email copy is to be relatable. To tell stories. To treat the email like it's written to their best friend. It shouldn't be written any differently than if it was an email to a good friend that you haven't talked to in six months.

It's totally your preference if you write long copy or want to write short copy. Short copy tends to get more clicks, but those clicks are less qualified. Long copy tends to get fewer clicks, but the clicks are highly qualified (they read your whole email!).

Step 4: Getting The Clickthrough

Now for the link you include in your email...

Your goal in writing an email is to get folks from your list back to your website for some reason. Sometimes, it's just to place a retargeting pixel or watch a video. Other times, it's because you're selling something.

At the end of the day, the link text you use in your email has a LOT to do with how many people click through.

Here are a few of the strategies we use in our emails from time to time. We switch it up here and there, depending on what looks better in the email copy.

Getting The Click

The subject line is the reason that someone opens your email. It makes sense to use the same text as your link.

For example, if your subject line is '7 Fat Burning Foods,' use it as the link in your email, taking prospects to watch the sales video!

Include A Clickable Image

Putting an image in your email content is a great way to encourage a clickthrough AND it helps your deliverability.

In order for someone to see the image, they have to enable images in some email platforms, which means they've taken another step in receiving your email…

That's a good thing!

Here are some types of images that you can include:

- A graphical button that they can click
- A screenshot of the page that they'll be going to after they click
- A banner that you plan on using for the page (think banner images like Facebook uses)
- A still image of the video that they'll be watching

Most times, you can just take a screenshot or some graphical element of the page that you're linking to to make this work!

The "Double Line Link Trick"

One of my favorites is the "Double Line Link."

In your body copy, a double line link is awfully hard to ignore. So, rather than use something like:

Click here >>

You use something like this:

Click here to download the 100 Most Opened

Subject Lines Report >>

If you do those links in blue, they are hard not to notice, so you'll get a bump in clicks!

List-Style Link Trick

Another thing I like to do from time to time is put a series of links in a list, all linking to the same place.

Oftentimes, I'll tie this to a 'rule' that saves the link that someone clicked so I can use it later for more specialized email copy.

For example, you can do something like this:

In the blog post, you'll discover:

- How to write subject lines that get the open.
- Crafting email body copy that gets read and clicked!
- Effectively preframing your prospect into buying before they ever get to your sales page…

Then, every link links right to the same place!

Spell It Out

This option is definitely the easiest…

Just spell out exactly what you want your prospect to do! The most obvious example is:

Click here >>

Or…

Download this PDF >>

You don't have to be fancy… Just get the click!

Some Additional Email Copywriting Tips

Here are some additional tips and tricks to writing email copy which'll make it easier for you to get done.

These tips are all tried and true, and have helped me immensely in getting more done in less time!

Write Narrow Email Copy

One little trick is that you don't ever have a line that is any more than 45 or 50 characters. Once the line gets to 45 or 50 characters you hold 'shift' and 'enter' and you just space the new line down.

It's just a single space, but that keeps people reading down the screen, no different than why a newspaper has multiple columns. It's really easy to just scan a newspaper and your email should be the same thing.

Batch Your Writing

Another tip is to batch copy when writing autoresponders. It helps you consciously open and close loops, sometimes between three or four emails.

Basically you start telling a story or you raise some sort of an objection in the first email, and then leave it open for a while. You don't answer that objection or finish that story until three or four emails later. This process opens a 'hook' in the reader's brain, and they have to close it by continuing your emails!

The important thing is that you're writing all of them in one stream of consciousness, so you're not getting up and moving around and constantly being interrupted. You write your emails while you're in the same train of thought, and you keep a consistent flow in your dialogue from email to email.

This ensures that you are very consistent in your speech patterns, the way you're talking and in the stories you're telling because you're doing it all in one sitting.

Include Bonding Emails

Another important thing to realize is that not every email has to be about selling. We call them bonding emails inside Scriptly.

I personally like to do three or four bonding emails as soon as somebody signs up for my list. The bonding sequences contain little promotional stuff, just a little bit, but establish a good common ground between the reader and me.

Lately, they've all been about bonding because we haven't sold anything inside the marketing niche, but other niches are a different story.

Turning Leads Into Sales

There's no better time than now to start ramping up your landing pages and dialing in your autoresponder, preparing for the new business that's about to come your way!

In this chapter, we're going to talk about some new lead generation and closing strategies that'll help dial in your campaigns. Plus, clue you in on some lead generation template ideas.

1. Use Quizzes to Ramp Up Your Leads

Because so much of our lives as marketers depend on the amount of fresh leads coming in, it's important to have a variety of tactics for reaching people. Those fun quizzes that pop up on your social media feed from time to time are actually great lead generation tools. Quizzes are a powerful tool when harnessed correctly and used to drive real leads that turn into actual revenue.

To learn how to use our high-conversion quiz and survey tool, check out:

http://askly.org/

2. Growing Your Business with Email Marketing Templates

Which templates generate the best engagement? What kind of 'asks' will get you closer to your goals? Email marketing is a great way of getting your prospects to take action, after they sign up onto your list…

That's why we created Scriptly – to help you write bulletproof email sequences that'll engage your prospects and help you sell more stuff!

Learn more about it here: **scriptly.org**.

3. Strategies to Personalize Your Upsells and Cross-Sells

Would you like fries with that? Research shows that upsells and cross-sells count for more than 30% of eCommerce revenue. As shoppers, we are accustomed to the standard sales tactics. Companies have more products. And they want us to buy more. The problem arises when brands force us to buy services we don't want.

Here are five strategies you can use to add upsells and cross-sells into your mix:

Focus on Timing and Limitations

It's 50% easier to sell to existing customers than to find new ones, so focus on them first.

Upsell to your customers when it makes the most sense, based on what they recently purchased from you and how they answer when you survey them.

Add User-Generated Content

Encourage your customers to post reviews of your products and share them on social media.

Facebook ads work very well for some businesses partly because they have these social elements built in, such as the ability to like, share, and comment on a post that you run as an ad.

Take a look at how amazon.com does things in this area, with user reviews, "people also liked," user-created lists, and other cross-selling techniques.

Offer Personal Product Recommendations

Use words like *you* and *your* when cross-selling. This helps the customer visualize themselves with your products.

Personalize your marketing communications wherever possible. Notice how Amazon shows your name on the page when you are logged in. You can do the same with email messages.

Test Different Payment Options

If you're selling something that costs more than a few dollars, try offering a payment plan. A lot of customers can afford your product but may have cash flow problems that make it difficult to pay the entire price up front.

If you accept PayPal, look into their PayPal Credit program. As I'm writing this, they offer an option for six-month, interest-free financing for purchases over $99 for customers who are U.S. residents. This is great for you and your buyers. They are able to spread their payments out over six months, and you still get paid the full amount up front. PayPal collects the payments, so you don't have to worry about getting paid.

Create bundles of your products to get customers to buy more from you. These should be products that are also sold separately, so your customers can see how much they are saving when they purchase the bundle. If possible, price your bundle so the customer ends up getting at least one of the products free. If your products are digital, which means they cost little or nothing to deliver, there's no real reason not to give a good discount on the bundle.

For example, say you have three products priced at $37, $67, and $97. Purchased separately, the total would be $201. Price your bundle at something like $147, which would be almost 27% off. In your offer, tell the customer exactly how much they are saving.

Consider Selling When Offering Support

Sometimes when you're having a customer support conversation, the customer will mention a need or a problem that might be solved by one of your products or services. Don't be shy about mentioning that when it makes sense.

A good rule of thumb is to only do this if the customer is already happy. Trying to sell to someone who is upset is just going to make the problem worse.

4. Close Leads That Come in Through Cold Email Pitches and Advertising

Leads from outbound marketing (email prospecting and paid ads) are flowing, CPAs are dropping, lead quality is improving, but deals aren't closing. Time to freak out? No. Time to turn off advertising? Probably not. Time to go back into stealth mode and stop selling? NO!

The best way to sell depends on the type of lead. Here are some common types.

Contact Request

This person is a high-quality lead because they are looking to buy or at least seriously interested in learning more about what you offer. These leads should be your top priority. Try to respond to them within a few minutes whenever possible. Schedule a conversation with them ASAP.

Here's a sample email reply to send to them:

subject: Let's schedule time to talk tomorrow

Bob,

Thanks for signing up for the XYZ consult. I'm excited to connect.

Do any of these times work for you: 9 am, 1 pm, or 4 pm PT?

Let me know when works best, and I'll send a calendar invite.

Thanks,
Jason

Free Trial Signup

These leads can be tricky, since some of them are serious about becoming paying customers and some are just taking the trial because it's free.

I recommend always collecting credit card information when offering free trials and setting up the trial so it automatically rolls over to paid status when the trial ends. Of course you need to be up front and clearly explain that the card will be billed if the customer does not cancel before the trial ends. If you don't collect payment details when offering trials, you will get a lot of fake signups, people who aren't serious, and people who might want your service but don't have a credit card to pay for it.

This is essentially assuming the sale, and it will save you a lot of time in following up. You might choose to follow up only with those people who cancel their trials, to find out why they canceled and see if there is some other way of getting their business.

Content Signup

These leads are people who signed up for your email newsletter, to receive a download, or registered for a webinar. Some of these people are serious about buying, but many are just looking for more information.

You're probably best off just offering them additional content and letting them come to you when they're ready for more.

Regardless of which type of lead you have, make things easy for them.

Grow Your Email List

Every few months I'll read articles saying email marketing is close to dying. It all starts with people saying "the warnings were always here" then they'll go on saying email marketing is going to be replaced with some new way to boost sales.

But then, I'll see a pop-up asking me to subscribe to their newsletter…

Let's get one thing straight. You will always need to grow your email list. Email marketing isn't going anywhere, and it provides better results than social media marketing in most cases. Just think at it this way:

When people subscribe to your content, read your newsletter, then click the link to your website, they have a greater intent to buy than what you get from social media platforms. The more people you get from email marketing to your website, the more possible clients or buyers you have.

Email marketing isn't going to disappear overnight, so buckle up and start growing your email list.

Are blogs the easiest way to grow your email list?

It depends. While blogs don't work for all online projects, they have a really nice conversion rate for email lists because they provide you the means to get people interested and provide them with the best content from your niche.

So, how do you grow your email list with the help of a business blog?

Offer them something in return.

Let's say you provide social media services. To get people interested and grow your email list, you can't just write content and hope that people subscribe after they get done reading your blog post, but the better way is to offer them something in return for signing up.

Write up a lead magnet, a 10-page ebook on best social media practices or any other important topic, and offer it free to those who subscribe to your email list. Create a detailed report on the ROI from specific social media tactics with charts and important data and provide it to people in exchange for their email address. It doesn't have to be complicated, it just has to get them interested.

To grow that email list, you're going to want to put up a dedicated landing page that'll offer the freebie or implement a lead magnet plugin, in exchange for their email address. That way, when folks visit the page, they have one of two options… Sign up or leave!

Use CTAs as hooks for your email marketing strategy.

If you don't have the time or resources to write ebooks or reports, you can try to get people interested through the use of well-placed CTAs in your blog posts. My advice would be to create several calls to action images and insert them in your relevant blog posts.

Start looking at your blog categories and design at least one CTA for each active category. You can add the CTAs at the bottom of the post or use a timed pop-up to show them when the reader has finished reading the article.

Optimize your blog to grow your email list.

WordPress or any blogging CMS you may use will provide numerous ways you can customize the layout of your blog or website. You can add widgets, pop-ups, footers, and other ways to customize your blog and get people to sign up.

What to do: Spend some time and analyze your business blog layout. Search for heat maps services and see what are the most active parts for your blog. Using this information add subscribe forms or pop-ups to your layout. You can even add a permanent sign-up form in the footer of your blog.

We use tools like:

- Visual Website Optimizer (vwo.com)
- Picreel (picreel.com)
- Inspectlet (inspectlet.com)
- Hotjar (hotjar.com)

On almost any site we set up, whether we're driving paid traffic to it or not, we want to make sure that what we wants users to do – they actually do! Those four tools will give you insight into what readers are ACTUALLY doing rather than what you think they should be doing…

What NOT to do: Don't go to the dark side and fill your blog posts and pages with sign-up forms and pop-ups. If people have to close three pop-ups before they can access your content, they will give up almost instantly.

Experiment and see what you can achieve by customizing your blog layout. Keep a close eye on your traffic and ask for feedback.

Don't forget about internal links!

I read several niche blogs, and I can't help to wonder why aren't they linking their own content more.

You want to keep the visitor as much as you can on your website. Adding internal links is a great way to reduce your website bounce rate and get more page views. Think of it like this: **if a visitor spends more time on your website, the chances that he'll join your email list will increase.** It's not rocket science.

You can add links to other related blog posts in your articles or you can use related posts plugins.

Always try to interact with your readers.

If you want to grow your email list, just writing top-notch content won't be enough. If you don't interact with your readers, they won't be interested in interacting with you.

There are several ways to interact with blog readers.

Through blog comments. Low impact tactic, since you need someone to start a conversation in the first place. I keep seeing how people just "like and share" rather than leave a comment. To improve this, you may want to add Facebook comments to your website or other comment platforms.

With the help of blog contests. This is so easy to do. If you want to step it up and get people interested in your product, create a contest for your readers. Offer big discount vouchers, relevant books, or gadgets as prizes to get your blog readers interested.

Blog contests help you grow your email list in two big ways. You will get them to spend more time on your company blog thus increasing the sign-up chances (indirect) and by collecting their email when they participate in your contest (direct).

There are so many ways to grow your email list with the help of your company blog. I just listed a few but I'm sure you can think of more.

Rule-Based Email Automation

Behavior segmentation is the darling of the Internet marketing world right now, and for good reason.

By knowing what your prospects are doing and setting up systems that cater to their interests and movement, you're able to engage more of your audience by sending fewer emails, creating a boatload of new revenue for your company.

Today, what I want to share with you is how to start setting up your systems the right way, so you can engage with your list more effectively.

Truly, Scriptly's Autoresponder Engine was built for this. Regardless of what you sell, with the Autoresponder Engine, you're able to craft your emails intelligently, always catering to the individual subscribers in the different segments of your email list.

Before we get started though, there are a few things that you'll need, to pull off behavioral segmentation, or dynamic segmentation as it's sometimes called.

The first is an understanding of list segmentation, and how to put people in different lists or categories based on tags.

And the second, you'll need one of the more advanced email marketing platforms, like Infusionsoft or Ontraport. You can pull some segmentation off in Aweber and some of the others, but you're limited to major actions someone on your list takes – like purchases.

In Infusionsoft and OntraPort, you can put people in different lists based on a URL that they visit, a link that they click, or a way that they fill out a form.

Before get into the specific campaigns that you can use to set up your segmentation system, let's first go through what a trigger is.

Tripping Triggers

In order to move someone from one list to another, there needs to be an event, or a trigger, that happens.

When someone does this, they get added to this sequence. When they do that, they get added to that sequence.

That's not too complicated to figure out.

- When someone goes to a product sales page on your site, they're automatically added to the email sequence that promotes said product.

- If someone visits a thank you page on your site, it's because they just bought something. You'll want to deliver their product and sell them the next thing in your sales funnel.

- Or, if someone from your list watches Video #1 in your launch process, you want them to then get added to the sequence that promotes Video #2 (and taken off of the Video #1 sequence).

- Another example - if someone clicks a link in your email but doesn't watch the video on that page, you want to send them an additional email linking to the video (or asking them what happened!).

The possibilities are endless as to what you can do. The first thing to think about though are triggers that need to happen in order to accomplish what you're trying to do.

A trigger is an action that your user either takes or doesn't take. Some examples being:

- Clicking a link in an email
- Answering Question #4 of a survey this way
- Visiting a page on your website
- Opening an email
- Buying something (or opting in for something)
- Logging into your membership more than eight times
- Adding a product to a shopping cart but not buying
- Buying your front end product, but not your upsell.

In each of these situations, there are actions associated with your customers, and you can use those actions to smartly automate and segment your list.

How we do it is by setting up a rule.

Setting Up Automation Rules

The automation rule that you set up in your system is the recipe. It's the thing that says is what happens when an action is triggered.

Here are some examples:

- Your subscriber doesn't click a link in any three consecutive emails, they are then moved to the next affiliate promotion sequence (because they obviously weren't interested in that initial product)

- Your new customer buys your front-end product and your first upsell, but not your second one; so they are sent confirmation emails for the Front End Product and Upsell #1, and then moved to the promotional sequence for Upsell #2 (so they are reminded to buy).

- Someone clicks the 'Add To Cart' button on your sales page, visits your shopping cart page and doesn't buy, so they are automatically added to your Shopping Cart Abandonment Sequence until they do (and this can all be done with URL's, not additional opt-in forms).

To do this, you're going to want to set up the autoresponder emails first, then create the rules inside of your system, so that when they start firing, you're all set.

In Infusionsoft, you do it under the Campaign Builder. In OntraPort, you set it up under Contacts >> Rules.

(NOTE: It's worth saying that you can do a lot of the same things through banner retargeting as well! Banner retargeting is based on including and excluding audiences of people who visit your site, which means that you can follow the same sorts of rules to move people from on retargeting segment to the next.)

Automated Marketing

Your automated system is only as good as the sequences that you set up for your prospects to move through, based on the actions that they take.

So, inside Scriptly, we've done all of the leg work for you.

Product Sales Sequence

The Product Sales Sequence helps you set up the emails needed to sell your product to your list, based on high-open subject lines and highly clickable email body copy.

With it, you can send your list right to sales videos or long form sales letters, as well as advertorial-type landing pages.

You can also use it for multi-video launches, sending folks from one video to the next!

Whenever you want to promote a product, service or coaching program to your list, use this sequence.

Go here to get the Product Sales Sequence: **scriptly.org**

(Note: We also have a sequence that writes all of your product launch copy as well!)

Ascension Sequence

The Ascension Sequence is designed for customers who buy a product, but not the next upsell.

So, you use this when someone buys your front-end report or membership, but not one of your upsells. If they buy your front-end product, but not Upsell #1 or Upsell #2, you're going to deploy the Ascension Sequence.

If they buy your front end product and Upsell #1, but not Upsell #2, you're still going to use the Ascension Sequence. The only difference is you're going to set it up to sell Upsell #2!

Go here to get the Ascension Sequence: **scriptly.org**

Shopping Cart Abandonment

The Shopping Cart Abandonment Sequence isn't particularly sexy, but it is powerful. With this sequence, you'll want to tag everyone who adds a product to the shopping cart, and then fire this email series when they don't buy after 24 hours.

So, your rule will be something like:

1. If prospect adds product to cart, put them in the Shopping Cart Abandonment Sequence.
2. When prospect buys, move them out of the Shopping Cart Abandonment Sequence.
3. If they are still there after 24 hours, start sending them email reminders, until they buy.

Follow?

Go here to get the Shopping Cart Abandonment Sequence: **scriptly.org**

Waiting List Relaunch Sequence

The Waiting List Relaunch Sequence is used when you close your offer or your launch, based on a countdown timer or class starting or whatever.

Usually, what happens is you'll put up a landing page that says, "This offer is closed."

When someone signs up on that page, they should be put into your Waiting List Relaunch Sequence. Email #1 thanks them for being added to the Waitlist. Email #2 through #5 invite them into the course and then shuts it down again.

You can modify the delay between email #1 and email #2 to be however long you wish :0)

Go here to get the Waiting List Relaunch Sequence: **scriptly.org**

Flash Sale Sequence

The Flash Sale Sequence is used when someone clicks a link to your sales letter, but doesn't buy at full price. Or, you can use it to re-engage your list. Or, you can use it just because.

The idea with a flash sale is that you get a bunch of new buyers for your discounted front end product, and then you march them through an upsell funnel to make some of that money back.

Which means, you can use the Ascension Sequence for the products that folks don't buy in your funnel!

Go here to get the Flash Sale Sequence: **scriptly.org**

Re-Engagement Sequence

The Re-Engagement Sequence acts like it sounds. If someone hasn't done anything for a certain number of days, they should get this email set.

These emails employ some of the best email subject lines and body copy that we've ever tested. Their importance is to get an old subscriber 'woken up' and clicking links again.

We also use this sequence to build credibility and some social proof, by showing them around the Internet a little bit and tying our brand with other HUGE brands.

Go here to get the Re-Engagement Sequence: **scriptly.org**

Post-Webinar Emails

After someone signs up for a webinar, it's pretty common to mail the replay video out to your new list.

What the Post-Webinar Email Sequence does is add a twist to it. We push the sale. Pretty hard.

If someone signed up for your webinar and either attended or didn't, we want to make sure that they have every possible opportunity to buy your offer. And after running hundreds of webinars, we've perfected the replay sequence many times over.

Typically, whatever sales you got on your webinar – you'll double that with this sequence going out within 24 hours of the webinar.

Go here to get the Post-Webinar Email Sequence: **scriptly.org**

Pre-Webinar Emails

The Pre-Webinar Emails are what you'll send to your list to promote your webinar. Meaning, after you decide to do a webinar, you'll queue this series up in your autoresponder and just let it go.

From a behavioral segmentation standpoint, there isn't much going on with this ones, unless you're moving someone off of a sequence that promotes a video, to a sequence that promotes a webinar. (Some folks would rather buy on a webinar!)

The key to these emails is to really spell out the benefits that someone will receive by attending!

Go here to get the Pre-Webinar Email Sequence: **scriptly.org**

Survey Sequence

Usually, if we find that someone isn't opening emails or clicking links for more than eight days, we'll add them to the Survey Sequence.

The idea is that if they were really interested in what we were talking about, they'd be doing something. If not, then we need to change course pretty quickly.

Now, I know that people's lives get hectic, and they aren't just sitting around waiting for an email from us, but if they're not doing anything, we try to figure out what kind of content they will be interested in.

So, we ask questions like, "What's Your Biggest Challenge?" and have them choose from a dropdown box.

Whatever they pick in the dropdown, they're automatically moved to a sequence catering specifically to the interests that they choose.

If we have products for that interest, then they naturally go through those first. If we don't, we put them in a sequence with affiliate offers.

Go here to get the Survey Sequence: **scriptly.org**

Bonding Sequence

The Bonding Sequence again, does like it sounds.

After someone signs up for your list, you have a very small window to make an impression on them and we do this by nurturing or bonding with them.

The bonding sequence typically goes out after your first product promotion, but before the next. So, in the overall scheme of things, this sequence is the second that they get added to.

What we want to do here is introduce them to us, what we stand for, who we are, and what we do. One of the things we do inside Scriptly's campaign to keep clicks up is link to social profiles, so they can get a good look at who we are!

Go here to get the Bonding Sequence: **scriptly.org**

Direct Revenue Sequence

Now, the Direct Revenue Sequence is probably my favorite, to this day. In this email autoresponder sequence, we ask a big question, much like the survey sequence, with one major difference.

We have them email us their answer.

What this does is open the door for coaching and consulting offers to be made through email or on the phone, and it's resulted in the fastest money I've ever made.

In fact, you'll see the Internet's top gurus doing similar stuff about once a month because it's such a revenue driver in their business.

Go here to get the Direct Revenue Sequence: **scriptly.org**

Wrapping Up

So, there you have it. Behavioral Ssquencing and the email templates that'll get it done for you. Now, it's your turn.

How do you plan on using these sequencing tips to generate more revenue?

Email Segmentation

Sending more email means making more money – right?

The old school of thought was that your email list should be treated like a hotel. Every day that goes by that you don't send an email, is wasted revenue.

Email frequency used to be treated like an opportunity that you can't get back – getting into your subscriber's inbox.

Now though, there's a much better way of managing your list that doesn't alienate your folks, and keeps your engagement and click rates steadily high.

Mailchimp did a study a few years ago, correlating frequency of emails and click rates. It turns out that the majority of folks in the study had diminishing click rates the more frequently they mailed.

Meaning, even though they were mailing more often, in some cases they were actually getting fewer overall clicks!

And really, you wouldn't believe how many product owners and email list owners I talk to who don't do any kind of list management whatsoever.

They have a big list, and they mail that big list!

They don't have any idea what their list is into or what they want more of. All they know is that at some point in the past, these subscribers opted in for something and they are just going to keep mailing.

When it comes to managing your lists, there are definite best practices that you should put in place, and it's important to understand that each list is different.

Things may work well for your list that don't work for others. In turn, you might hear people tell you what you need to do, and it might backfire.

So, know that you need to test this stuff out religiously and understand that your list might be a little different than everyone else's!

Knowing What Your List Wants

Email list management can be a pain sometimes. If you've got lots of products or websites, you've inevitably got quite a few lists that are segmented a million different ways and have lots of autoresponder sequences set up.

Keep in mind, your list is probably your company's most valuable asset, so invest some time into understanding what your folks want more of and what they can't stand!

Now, I know there are countless experts around the web trying to convince you that you need to build your list. But once you have it, what should you do?

Should you email them once a week? Should you write long emails? Should the content be formal or conversational? Should you put your logo at the top and make it look pretty? Should you hire someone to manage the list?

There are so many variables, and we'll be getting into them in a minute!

How To Properly Segment Your List

How you arrange your list matters. The person who has the best control over their list wins at the end of the day.

By segmenting your list the right way, you'll be sending less email on a daily basis while getting better engagement, higher clickthroughs, and more revenue!

Buyers vs. Prospects

Think about this. Who is a better prospect – someone who has bought from you in the past or someone who hasn't?

Someone who has bought from you, of course! They've shown you that they value your information or products or services or whatever. They're not afraid to buy something online. Plus, they have the resources to actually purchase something!

That means your buyer list should be your absolute most coveted list!

The folks who've never bought anything from you have a lower weight in terms of list value. Those folks found you for a variety of reasons. Maybe you gave away a free report or a piece of software or something, and they just signed up to get that something for free.

Realistically speaking, just having those two lists is a big deal. You'll treat your buyers and prospects differently. You might send something to your prospects that you don't send to your buyers and vice-versa.

So, at minimum, you should have a buyers list and prospects list.

Now, let's break them down even more.

Keeping Affiliates and JVs Separate

Affiliates and JVs are your marketing partners – they help you reach the corners of the Internet while making a percentage of the products and services sold.

For this reason, you should keep your affiliates on a separate list, making sure to only mail to them when you have something for them! Think affiliate contests, new products, launches, or you're moving in a new direction.

The ONLY market where your affiliate list might be your prospect list is in the Internet marketing space. You want your affiliates to be well-trained so that they can help you promote better, so it would be advantageous to do some training or link to good marketing products.

I know quite a few product owners in different niches who have entire courses that they give away for free to their affiliates, all in hopes of making them better marketers!

List Interests

Let's face it, not every person on your list is interested in the same thing. In the Internet marketing space, some folks are interested in free traffic. Others in paid traffic. Still others in list building or product development.

The more control you have over what your list is interested in, the better you can market to them.

There are quite a few ways that you can figure this out…

- Surveying your list
- Monitoring email link clickthroughs and assigning them to a tag
- Putting a dropdown list on the opt-in form
- Tracking what pages someone visits and putting them in different tags

There are lots of ways to get this data. I like easier things than just surveying the list.

If I mail my list of 40,000 business owners, with some clicking through and then some filling out the survey, I have a very poor picture of what my list is into, simply because there isn't enough data!

If, however, I track who opened an email based on the subject line, I'll have a much better idea of what they want more of!

Some email platforms like Ontraport and Infusionsoft make this type of behavioral segmentation pretty easy.

Active vs. Inactive Leads

With email, on most platforms including Ontraport, you have to pay once you hit a number of emails sent.

For example, included in the monthly cost is the ability to send 100,000 emails. Once we hit that 100K cap, we pay $99 for each additional 100K emails sent.

There are months we'll spend another $1200 on email! Crazy, huh?

Plus, if you send email to folks who don't open them, it hurts your deliverability rates. One time I hit the wrong button and only about 55% of my email was actually delivered. (Email deliverability is important.)

One way to curb both of those things, extra costs and low deliverability rates, is to only send email to your active subscribers.

Let's face it. If someone hasn't opened your email in the last four months, they probably aren't going to.

I know it hurts but just delete them out of your system. They're gone. And if they come back, they'll sign up for your stuff again.

If you can't bring yourself to delete them, then set their email status to 'No' or unsubscribe them or whatever.

How Did They Find You?

Oftentimes, I'll segment our lists by what promo they signed up for, meaning which ebook did they download or which video they watched which make them sign up?

Another way I'll do it since we work with some affiliates is tag leads according to who sent them. It's fun to go through and see how many people are on how many lists!

In fact, when we were doing a lot of webinars a few years ago, fewer and fewer people were actually new to me! It got to the point where we'd run an import of the people who signed up and only about 30% were new leads!!

You wouldn't believe how many people signed up for the same webinar four or five times through different affiliates. (Maybe you were one of them? – there's nothing wrong with that by the way!)

Additional List Management Tips

Here are some additional list management tips that have worked for me.

Email Your List Often

The first time I heard this, I almost laughed. If I email my list everyday, people will unsubscribe! They'll report my emails as spam. I worked so hard to get them on – I don't want to piss them off!

What I can tell you is that the people who unsubscribe would have done so anyway, sooner or later. There's no way you can continue to give away content week after week without asking them to take action in some way. Maybe that's through an affiliate link or by selling your own products.

The point is, you're in business to make money, right? That's what keeps the lights on and a roof over your head. Your true prospects, friends, and customers will understand that.

Make Use Of Actions And Rules

In some of the more sophisticated email marketing platforms, like Ontraport and Infusionsoft, you can do lots of complex segmentation.

Things like:

- If someone goes to this page, add them to this list
- If someone clicks this link, remove them from List 1 and put them on List 2
- If someone chooses this field in this form, add them to this sequence
- If a customer buys X product, put them in the sequence that promotes Y product

The term 'behavioral segmentation' seems to be the newest phrase in Internet marketing, and the examples above are what's fueling that revolution.

My point is, the better you understand what your list is doing and what they're into, the fewer emails you can send and the greater your engagement will be!

Keep Things Current

If you don't plan on writing to your list every day or every couple days, set up an autoresponder series that does it for you. That's why we built Scriptly, to make autoresponders easy.

The worst thing you can do is let people forget who you are.

Actually, just this morning, I got two emails – one from Tony Robbins with a direct link to a video and one from another email marketer with an opt-in which forwarded me to the same video.

Keep in mind, this is the first email I got from the no-name marketer and I was a bit skeptical. I didn't remember signing up for anything of his. I didn't recognize his name at first. And I was a bit weirded out because he was making me signup for something I already had a link to. I thought maybe he was trying to grow his list off of Tony's video.

So, after twenty minutes of checking nameservers and digging, I finally remembered who this guy was (and it's cool…). I just didn't remember what I was doing on his list!

Why Your Traffic Isn't Converting

Building an email list is both highly profitable, and one of the only assets that you'll ever have in an online, digitally-driven business.

What your list does is insulate you from a lot of the changes that happen online, from ad networks not playing nice to Google deciding to update its algorithm and stop sending all that traffic to you.

By learning how to get folks to raise their hands and say, "I want to learn more from you," you're adopting one of the most tried and true business-building strategies online, and you can market to them anytime you like!

That means, you can send out product promotions, webinar promotions, and flash sales… All at the drop of a hat!

Take a few minutes and carefully go through these five insights. They'll be key in really scaling your business.

Getting Your First 100 Email Subscribers (The Easy Way)

If you want to maximize your business' profit, there's one thing you need to know: email marketing has a return on investment (ROI) that beats any alternative—by a lot. I mention it fairly often, so you might already know that. But then why haven't you started?

Here is the industry average ROI per $1 spent on various methods:

Email - $40
Catalogs - $7.30
SEO - $22.24
Internet display - $19.72
Mobile - $10.51
Keyword ads - $17
Banner ads - $2

Here are the steps to follow.

Start with one great piece of content. Figure out something that would really resonate with your audience and write a blog post about it. The idea is to establish you as a thought leader in your niche, someone people should pay attention to.

Two types of posts that are well-suited for this purpose are

* Detailed list-based posts
* Definitive guide to some topic

A good place to search for ideas is forums. Look for questions people ask over and over. A post answering these questions in detail would be a good way to attract an audience.

Another place to search is your competitors' websites and blogs. What topics are they writing about? If their site allows comments, which articles are getting lots of comments?

A third place to look for ideas is Reddit, which allows its users to vote on posts. The more votes a post gets, the more popular it is. Look at popular posts for ideas on what to write about.

Once you have a great idea, spend some time writing your great post. Several hours, at least. This is not the type of post to crank out in a few minutes.

Put some effort into the design of your post. Add graphics to make it more understandable and attractive. Use formatting like bold and italics where appropriate. Include subheadings to break your text into shorter chunks.

Important: Don't publish this post yet.

The second major step of this process is to create a lead magnet which takes your new post and expands on it or is otherwise very relevant to the post. The idea is to get your readers so excited when they read the post that they want the lead magnet, too.

Create a separate opt-in page on your blog for this new lead magnet.

Create a box offering the lead magnet and place it inside the article, once near the top and again near the bottom. This can be as simple as a sentence or two describing the lead magnet and linking to the opt-in page for it. Use a different background color for the box, like light blue or yellow, so it stands out.

Now it's time to publish the new post.

The next step is to get traffic to the post, so you can get some subscribers from it.

Here are a few free traffic sources:

- Forums: Find some good ones in your niche, make useful posts, then (if allowed) include a link to your blog post in some of your forum posts. Some forums won't allow that but will allow a link in your signature.
- Reddit and similar sites: Write a detailed summary of your blog post, including a link to it, and post on the site.
- Guest posting: Write guest posts for other blogs and include a link to the opt-in page you created for your special blog post. Be sure that's allowed before you submit the guest post.
- Facebook, Twitter, and other social media: If you have any following on these sites, post a brief summary of your special blog post, including a link to it.

The next major step is to have a plan for emailing your new subscribers. Too many site owners do the work of getting signups, then waste them by not emailing their list.

Write a welcome email that all new subscribers receive right away and a few other followup messages to be sent out every few days. You can include quality content, surveys, and links to some of your other blog posts in these messages.

You can use Scriptly to help you with some of these messages: **scriptly.org**

The main idea is to get your new subscribers used to hearing from you so they don't forget who you are.

Be sure to keep building your list by writing more quality posts and getting more traffic to them.

How to Use the Word "Free" Without Losing Credibility

Marketers use the word "free" so often that it has nearly lost its power. Free is a word that has enormous psychological appeal. But when it's overused or used incorrectly, it can ruin your marketing efforts. Here's how to use the word *free* for conversion power, marketing advantage, and increased revenue.

Free is powerful in marketing because of reciprocity. This is the feeling that if someone does something for you, you should do something for them.

Think of stores that give out free samples, like restaurants in the mall food court. The simple act of getting something free compels some people to purchase from that business, even if it's not the same item they sampled.

The problem with reciprocity is that it's so powerful that it can turn into guilt. People might feel guilty if they get the freebie and don't buy anything, so some will turn down the gift to avoid the feeling of guilt.

One way to get around this is to explain why you're giving away the item. The most common explanation is that you want to let people sample what you have to offer because you know some of them will like it enough to buy it.

That's why there are free samples of bourbon chicken in the food court and why many software services offer free trials.

Maybe you have another reason for your freebie; if so, just explain what that is.

Another thing you can do is have a free offer alongside paid ones. Say you own a membership site that people pay a monthly fee to access. You could create another level of the site that is free and offers less content or fewer benefits than your paid level. The idea is to get people into the free level, knowing that some will upgrade to paid to get those extra benefits.

That's a very common arrangement with business software. The software might be free for X number of uses per month, than after that there is a fee. An autoresponder service might offer free accounts for people who have fewer than 500 subscribers. They know that once your list grows beyond that size, you'll still need their service, so if they can get you in the door with a free account, there's a good chance you will eventually upgrade.

If you use this strategy, make a comparison chart showing the benefits for free and paid users so people can see what they get.

Don't overdo it with the word *free*. It will attract some people who will never become paying customers and may be more difficult to please.

Make sure your free offer still has quality. People won't appreciate your freebie if it lacks value. When creating it, put in the same effort you would use if you were planning to charge for it.

HTML vs Plain Text Emails

A key decision to make for your email marketing campaigns is whether to use plain text emails or HTML messages. HTML lets you make your email look more like a web page or a page from a magazine. However, HTML formatting can take lots of time and if not done correctly, may look weird in some email programs. Also, many email programs have HTML and images turned off by default, so your HTML messages really look bad for many of your subscribers.

The great thing about plain text email, besides the ease of using it, is that every email reader on every device, no matter how basic or sophisticated, can display the message in a way that's easy to read and looks good.

This is a decision you'll have to make for yourself. Most one-person businesses I know use plain text, because it's faster and easier. HTML messages tend to be used by most bigger companies. A company like Amazon, Best Buy, or Walmart almost always use HTML emails. Of course they can also afford to have full-time employees who do nothing but design and write their email messages.

Use a Clean Layout

If you do decide to go with HTML, my advice is to keep it simple. A three-column design with fancy sidebars can look beautiful on a web page, but in email can be hard to read. More and more people are using their mobile phones to read their email, and your fancy, multi-column design might be barely readable on those smaller screens.

I would stick with a one-column design so the body of your message uses the full width of the email program. This makes it easier on the reader regardless of which device they are using.

Images in Your Emails

Although it's nice to put images in your blog posts, you generally don't need to use them in the body of your emails, unless there's something really essential in the graphic that you can't easily state in words. For example, a photo of your physical product.

If you have fancy charts, graphs, or infographics, those would be more suited for use in blog posts than in your emails. Use the email message to promote the blog post rather than cramming the graphic into the email itself.

The two graphics you might want to use in your HTML emails are the header and footer. The header can include the name of your newsletter or company, and the footer can include your signature, photo or logo (if not already in the header), and contact information.

The same goes for elements like fancy fonts. I've seen a few people use complicated or elegant fonts like cursive in their emails. These fonts might look great on a wedding invitation or fancy restaurant menu, but in an email message, they are annoying and hard to read. You want to make the text in your emails as easy to read as possible. Your words are what are going to get people to take action (make a purchase, click a link, etc.), much more so than a pretty-looking design.

By sticking with a simple, one-column design, your HTML emails will be more readable on more devices and much less work for you to produce. Once you find a design you like, use it consistently. One of the purposes of elements like graphic headers is for branding, which works better if you keep it consistent.

Other Factors in Emails

Make sure the calls to action in your emails are visible and obvious. Use white space around them so they stand out. Too many companies use complex graphics with clickable parts that are not at all obvious that you're supposed to click on them. That's a great way to not get clicks.

If you use a clickable image like a button in your email, also include the same link in text format for people who have images turned off.

Ways to Boost Your Conversions

Do you struggle with writing features and benefits? Things that are really telling about what you're offering or what you want someone to opt-in for?
Here are some thoughts on that:

1. Make Your Sales Pages Easy to Navigate

Some tips:

- Get rid of excess categories, useless labels, and multiple tabs.
- Have a clear call to action and make it easy to find. (Hint: if you have order buttons or links in the middle of the page, be sure to put one at the bottom, because that's where many users will go to find them.)
- Use bulleted lists for your benefits. (Like this one.)

2. Make Your Calls to Action Compelling

Remember that it's your words that get people to click your order button, not your fancy page design.

Don't be afraid to tell people exactly what you want them to do, using a strong call to action. Include some urgency in your statement. If your bonuses are expiring, your offer is ending, or your price is rising soon, include that in your call to action.

Example: **Click the button below to get the ABC Diet and start shedding pounds before we take away the meal plan bonus.**

Be honest in your statements. Don't say the price is going up or the offer is ending soon if it's not. That erodes trust in you if the visitor comes back after your supposed deadline and the offer is still the same. It can also get you in legal trouble.

What if there's nothing time-sensitive about your offer? You can still add urgency to your CTA in an ethical way. Focus on the benefits of buying your product or service and remind your visitor that the sooner they purchase, the sooner they will get the results they want.

Example: **Click the button below to get the ABC Diet and start shedding pounds in time for beach season.**

In that example we're using the changing seasons as a reason to act now. That would be a great CTA to use in the winter or spring months. Just make sure to change it by summer, since if someone sees that in August, they will be confused. You could change the last part of it to something like **before summer ends** or **in time for the holidays** or **before the new year starts**.

If you don't want to make your CTA that seasonal, here's an example that you could use all year: **Click the button below to get the ABC Diet and start shedding pounds right away.**

Think about it. If someone wants to lose weight and thinks your product will help them, shouldn't that be enough reason to buy now? In the long run, the price of the program isn't nearly as important as the person looking and feeling better, improving their health, etc.

If you don't mind getting just a little negative, you can inject some pain into your CTA, like this: **You won't shed those pounds until you take action. Click the button below to get the XYZ Diet and start getting results right away.**

Don't feel bad about doing that. All you're really doing is pointing out something your reader is already thinking. If your product works, you're doing them a favor by giving them a push to buy now.

You can easily add urgency to any "how to" type product by pointing out that people won't get the results they want until they take action. That probably sounds obvious, but pointing it out can make a big difference.

3. Consider Offering Live Chat

Surveys show that customers love live chat features on websites, and software makes it easy to add that functionality to your site.

That's assuming you (or your staff) is going to be online during typical business hours to chat with people. If you have a full-time job and are a one-person business, you probably don't have the time to do this yourself.

You can train others to do this for you. You'll have to weigh whether the costs of doing this are worth it. If your site doesn't get a lot of traffic, there might not be enough chat requests to make it worth paying someone to be online and ready to chat (since you're going to have to pay them regardless of how busy they are).

If you have someone else run your chat, maintain a list of commonly-asked questions and suitable replies, so your chat person knows what to say. Have them keep track of any questions they get that they can't answer and add these to the list.

Live chat could be especially useful for you if any of these are true:

- Your site gets a lot of traffic or your sales volume is high.
- Your products or services are high-ticket or generate a lot of questions from prospects before they purchase (for example, coaching).
- You're already online most of the time your prospects would be asking questions or do enough business that the cost of having someone chat with prospects for you is not a big deal.

Offering live chat can be a big boost to your business. Just make sure if you add it to your site, someone is around to answer the questions that come in. A chat feature that is always off is worse than none at all.

4. Implement Split Testing

Split testing is one of the most effective ways of improving your conversions, but most people don't bother doing it, because they don't know how or they think it's too hard.

There are several varieties of split testing. Let's focus on the simplest, known as A/B split testing.

All this means is having two versions of your page and seeing which one gets a higher conversion rate over time. The first visitor is shown page A, the second is shown page B, the next person sees page A, etc. Usually cookies are used so the person is shown the same version of the page they saw last time if they come back to your site.

The technical details of how to implement this are beyond the scope of this book, so I will explain how it works in general. You need split testing software to set this up, and the details of that depend on which software you use, another reason I can't get too deep into it here.

To make your split test valid, only change one element at a time, such as the headline. The rest of your page should be the same. If you change the headline, background color, order button, and price all at the same time, and one version of the page performs much better than the other, you'll never be able to tell which specific change made the difference.

You need to take a logical, emotionless approach to split testing. Let the results be your guide. Let's say your sales page has been up for a while. Let's call that original version A. Make a copy of it, change one element like the headline, and call that version B.

Next you need to be patient. You need to have a certain number of conversions before you can truly tell which version performed best. Your split testing software documentation should explain how long to run your test and show you how valid the results are. There is a concept in statistics called confidence. This is expressed as a percentage. The longer your test runs, the closer the confidence will get to 100%.

For example, your software might show that version A converted at 1.2%, version B converted at 1.6%, with a confidence of 86%. That means there is an 86% chance that version B will outperform version A in the long run. You'll have to decide how high a confidence level to shoot for before you stop the test and accept the results. I like to shoot for at least 90%.

What matters with split testing is not how much time elapses, but how many actions (visits, sales, etc.) take place. This means if your site gets a low amount of traffic, your test will have to run for a long time to be statistically valid. It could take weeks or longer. A high-traffic site like Amazon can run a valid test in minutes if not seconds.

This is why patience is so important. The biggest mistake people make with split testing (other than not doing it at all) is not letting their tests run long enough and making decisions based on incomplete data. That can lead you to choosing the wrong version of your page as the winner.

Let's say you have a low-traffic site and get 20 visitors a day, 10 each to version A and B. The first day, your site converts very well, and version A makes 2 sales, while B makes 1 sale.

Those are conversion rates of 20% and 10%, which are awesome for most products but unlikely to last long term. Two out of 10 visitors buying is more of a fluke than anything.

An impatient person might look at those numbers and think wow, version A performs twice as well as version B. That was true for that first day, but it's way too soon to conclude anything. If a baseball player hits a home run the first time he bats, no one would assume he's going to hit one every time. But if you compare two players over a full season, their batting averages are a pretty realistic statistic of how well they hit that year.

Once your test has run long enough and the confidence number is high enough for you, it's time to start another test. Let's say you're testing headlines, and version A performed better. I would come up with a third headline to test and make a version of the page with that. Call that version C. Now it's time to test A against C. Since B already lost, there is no need to use it again.

I suggest keeping a log of your test results. Record the dates of your test, details of what you were testing, and the results. Your software might keep track of these, but it's always good to have a backup. When it's time to create versions C, D, or E, check your log and make sure you don't accidentally use headline B again. The only version you should test again is the winning one.

The nature of split testing is that sometimes A will win, sometimes B will win. In other words, sometimes the newer version will do worse than the older one. Of course we want to find things that do better, but don't feel bad when the new one does worse. Just like the baseball player that knows he won't hit a home run (or even a single) every time, realize that sometimes the older version will do better. All you really need to do is make sure you keep track of your all-time best performing version (which in copywriting circles is called the control), and always test that against something new.

Running A Profitable Flash Sale

Way back when I worked at Pepsi, we used to run flash sales on close-dated pop (AKA soda in most of the country).

Whenever we found something that was close to going out of date, we'd slap a sticker on it for 50% off and push it in a cart up to the registers in the front.

Within a few days, all the close-dated pop would be gone, and I didn't have a manager breathing down my neck anymore. Problem solved.

The very first time I got an email announcing a flash sale, that's what I thought of. And since then, it seemed that everyone and their brother was doing these 'timed sales', which tells me one thing...

They work!

So, we started running our own, in lots of different niches and on lots of different products. All with fantastic success!

And when you think about it, Groupon and Woot have used this idea of a flash sale to build their entire business model! And don't get me started on Black Friday... Black Friday is a collection of flash sales, all day long!

I share all this to say...

Flash sales should be a part of what you do. There are plenty of benefits to a flash sale, and by the end of this chapter you'll have a great idea of how to get one launched in your business.

Why Flash Sales Work

The whole goal of a flash sale is to get a prospect to take action, using scarcity and discounts as the motivational tools behind it.

If you know you only have three days to make a purchase for an extreme discount, then each day that passes makes your action more and more urgent – if you want what they're selling of course!

For instance, over the weekend, Woot had a FitBit wristband for sale. I saw the email, but didn't take action. I logged in this morning (knowing of course that it'd be gone), and it was.

And I kicked myself for not checking the site sooner!

The same thing will happen with your customers. They'll understand that you're giving them a HUGE discount. They'll know that they have a few days to buy. If they don't, they lose out!

Fear of loss is a very powerful motivator.

Now, there's a reason why we see flash sales all over the place. Honestly, it's not about the income they produce (especially if you're selling a digital product).

If you have a video course that's $47 and you discount it to $7 for a three-day flash sale, that's a big break for your customers. But… If you sell 100 copies, you've only made $700.

The REAL reason you run flash sales is to get more of your customers into an upsell funnel. (They are also great for raising the clickthrough rates of your emails.)

If you have a $7 front end offer and then the next offer in the upsell funnel is $47, you might have 30% or 40% who take you up on that!

And, if there's a second upsell at $197, you might have 10% who take you up on that!!

So, the $7 front end product is really more about qualifying buyers than anything else, and moving them through your upsell process. If you want to move more of your prospects to buyers – run a Flash Sale!

Closing the Flash Sale Down

At the end of the flash sale, you need to shut it down.

That means you can stay up until when it's done and redirect the page, or you can employ any one of the countdown widgets to redirect the page for you.

Personally, I use a landing page template which has a countdown widget as part of it. Once the clock hits zero, the page redirects somewhere else. Usually, to a "Thanks, but you missed it!" page.

You might get some emails about extending the sale for a customer due to some special case, but that's for you to make the call on.

You just want to make sure that publicly, the page is closed when you say it's going to be! Otherwise, you lose credibility and people think your sale wasn't a sale, just a trick to get them to your site.

Executing Your Flash Sale

There are four steps to running a highly profitable, highly motivating flash sale.

They aren't tricky and most of the complicated work is probably already done for you...

Really, it'll involve changing the price of one of your products, figuring out how long your flash sale should be in place for, and letting your audience know about it!

Choosing Your Offer

You can choose any front-end product or service to do a flash sale with, but the best ones are always your newer offers or the one that stands out as your best.

If you're releasing something new into the market, a flash sale might be a great way to get it out there and generating some sales quickly, or...

If you've got a flagship, lower-end product that always serves as one of the best in terms of moving folks from being prospects to paid customers – use that one.

You want to be able to offer it at a substantial discount, so the publicly available price should be $37 or more.

Maybe you have a video course that sells for $67 or an ebook that sells for $47... It doesn't matter how much it normally sells for – you just want the discount to be pretty substantial!

Nothing gets people's attention more than an email email that says, "Get 80% off today!"

Putting a Time Limit in Place

When putting together your Flash Sale, make sure to put a time limit in place.

We've found that three days works the best for digital products, physical products, and software. If you're promoting a service, you might need a little longer.

One of the reasons we keep it to a multi-day process is to make sure that everyone on the list sees the email at least once. If we make it 12 hours or 24 hours, there's a good chance that folks on your list won't see it!

The three-day flash sale also allows for folks who aren't quite as diligent about checking their email or who are really busy.

At the end of the day, remember that every single one of the emails you send out is going to a real, live person who has their own commitments, obligations, and lives of their own!

Letting Your Audience Know

Of all the ways to drive traffic to a website, there are very few as dependable and quantifiable as sending out an email to your list!

Your email list is made up of people who have expressed interest in you and your products at some point in the past – it only makes sense that they'd be interested in a flash sale.

Use the flash sale announcement as a reason to communicate with them, even if you haven't had that much interaction with them recently.

You'll be surprised how many of your prospects will jump into your fold once they learn about the discount that you're giving (and the fact that it's going away in so many days!)

The Final Push

It's easy to forget sometimes, but the last email on the last day that you send is what will drive 70% of your sales…

Four or five hours before the promotion is set to end, email your list one last final reminder to jump in. You'll notice a steady stream of buyers come in the hours between when that email is sent and when the offer closes.

That means, more people in your upsell sequences where you can really start bumping up the average customer value of your buyers!

Launching Your Flash Sale

Inside Scriptly, there's a Flash Sale Autoresponder Template waiting for you to use.

It's a four-email, three-day template that you can use to promote a flash sale to your list. Included in the template are:

- Directions on when to mail it out
- The exact subject lines that have been proven to increase open rates
- Email body copy that's more effective in getting someone to click to a flash sale
- The "Final Push" email that engages your last minute shoppers

All you have to do is generate your flash sale template, copy and paste it into your autoresponder software, and you're all set to start mailing!

How To Sell Anything, Faster.

Over ten years ago, I got started online. That's interesting to think about because back when I got started, Facebook was non-existent. Myspace and Youtube were just being brought out. And I was desperately trying to figure out this thing called affiliate marketing.

It took me close to three years to really get good at affiliate marketing, and in the process, I learned tons of beneficial things...

Things like how to build websites, ranking websites in Google, driving traffic, and setting up systems.

I've probably built 600 websites and at a time controlled over 800 domain names – many of which I thought were awesome ideas to build, but never actually had a chance to.

The deeper I got into Internet marketing, the more I realized that selling and marketing online is exactly like selling and marketing in real life – with one major exception...

The medium is different.

Online, a nobody can have a following of tens of thousands, even hundreds of thousands of people.

You wouldn't know it to see him or her walking down the street – but that doesn't change the fact that it's true.

And being that the medium is different, so are the tools you use for the selling process.

Rather than sell one-to-one, you can sell one-to-many.

You don't need to drive down the street or into the neighboring town, have two or three meetings, and then (hopefully) get a sale...

Now, you can put hundreds of people on a webinar and sell them ALL at the same time without leaving your office!

At the end of the day, selling really only boils down to a few things...

You Must Solve a Problem

This goes without saying... You need to sell stuff that solves problems. The bigger the problem, the more you can sell.

There's a catch-22 there though. Sure, you might have the best solution on the planet, but you still need to make sure that you're out in front of your audience. The folks who are both willing and able to buy from you!

Many, many good products and services have died a slow death because the business owner didn't figure out how to get in front of the right market.

Know Your Audience

You have to know exactly who your ideal customer is (and who they aren't!). We can talk all day about defining your perfect customer avatar, but at a minimum, you should know:

- Their gender
- How old they are
- What they do for a living
- What they're interested in
- Where they live
- What languages they speak
- What devices they use

That, my friends, just gets you started. In order to write sales copy and really make them feel like you're talking to them, you should have a pretty good idea about:

- What they do in their free time
- What their biggest aspirations are
- What they fear the most
- What they eat
- What time they wake up / go to bed
- What they enjoy doing on vacation
- What kind of car they drive

In short, you should know so much about this person, that you should give them a name. And, every time you sit down at your desk to write anything even remotely sales related, you should be trying to figure out how to best communicate with "Bob" (or Mack or Angela or Buddy).

To make this easier, we included a customer avatar builder inside Scriptly that'll help you pinpoint your ideal client, and use that data to speak directly to them through emails and webinars!

Create a <u>Structured</u> Sales Process

The Internet and what it has done for business folks like us is pretty marvelous, but the absolute biggest advantage we have now is in how easy it is to create a structured sales process.

Between having dedicated sales mechanisms like webinars, sales videos and email autoresponders; it's relatively easy to create a standalone sales process in your business that welcomes every new lead in while funneling revenue out.

That's why we created Scriptly – to make it easy to handle all of the copy that needs to be in place to make that happen.

Sure, you might still need sales people but the people they do talk to will be much more qualified!

The Call to Action Must Be Clear

Every piece of content, every blog post, every Facebook post, and every email that goes out to you audience should have a clear call to action in it.

And if it doesn't, you need to have a reason why it wasn't included.

Now, I'm not talking links to just sales messages either. You should always ask your audience to do something like:

- Clicking a link to watch a Youtube video.
- Signing up for your next webinar.
- Liking a new blog post.
- Subscribing to your Youtube channel.
- Opting in for a new report.
- And, of course, clicking a link to go check out a sales video

Inside Scriptly, you'll find everything from bonding sequences to product sales sequences and the common element between them ALL is that we're asking audiences to take action.

Every email is structured so that they <u>A) get opened, B) get read, and C) get</u>

224

<u>clicked</u>.

Which leads me to the last part... Creating systems.

Systematize Your Process

I'm a big believer in systems. Why? Having built hundreds of them for clients and for my businesses... Having a system, or a machine, that turns leads into sales is the absolute most powerful thing in business. When you can spend a dollar and get back two – you're onto something big!

To this day, one of the most profitable systems to employ is a webinar:

- Your new leads sign up for your webinar
- On the webinar, you bond with them, teach them, and ultimately pitch them (resulting in some sales)
- After your webinar, you mail them a replay of the presentation (getting more sales)
- After four or five days, you shut down the webinar replay (which results in another sales spike)
- And then you have a bunch of leads to mail your next offer!

To help you along the process, not only does Scriptly have a webinar writer, called the Webinar Wizard... We also have the webinar promotion email sequence AND the replay email sequence that you can use for your promotion! In fact, we include four webinar sequences, promotional and replay sequences for evergreen offers and for time-limited offers. So if you're running an automated webinar, your offer is not closing anytime soon, and you don't want to say in your emails that it's ending, we've got you covered.

All that's left for you to do is set it up in your autoresponder! Or, if you'd like us to do it for you, you can tell us about your project at **DoneForYou.com**.

Promoting Affiliate Products

In this chapter we're going to get into exactly what affiliate marketing is, what it isn't, and what you can expect when you get started.

By the end of this tutorial, you'll know why companies pay affiliates handsomely for sending traffic to them, how to find affiliate offers that you can promote, and how to cash out by promoting other people's products.

The beauty of being an affiliate is that most of the overhead in building a business is taken care of for you – you send traffic and you get paid a portion of all the sales that happen as a result of that traffic.

It's a beautiful model, and one I know very well since it's how I got my start!

What Is Affiliate Marketing?

When it comes to making money online, there are two different ways you can go about it. You can either:

1. Sell somebody else's products or services
2. Sell your own products and services

Affiliate marketing is best described as: **Selling Other People's Stuff**.

Being an affiliate, or selling somebody else's products, is a lot easier to get started with overall. When you promote another product or another company, they do all the hard work. They write the sales copy. They maintain their product. They do customer service and merchant processing…

And you, as an affiliate, get a check in the mail! Or more likely, a PayPal payment or electronic deposit to your bank account.

For you, it's pretty hands off. You promote a product online and get paid!

How to Promote Affiliate Products

There are tons of ways to promote affiliate products, some more difficult than others. For the purposes of this tutorial, because most everyone who's reading it are Scriptly members, we're going to concentrate on one of the easiest and most profitable ways of getting started...

Email marketing.

With email marketing, all you have to do to promote an affiliate product is send an email to your list.

Some people will open your email. Some will click on your affiliate link. And some will buy the product!

When someone buys the product, you get paid your affiliate commission!

Before we get into the process, let's talk about why a company will pay an affiliate like you and me.

Why Do Companies Pay Affiliates?

The simple explanation is that people and companies pay millions of dollars every day to folks like you and me to help them sell their products and services online.

These companies are smart.

They know that the Internet is a big place and it's way easier to pay you to recommend their products to your friends, family and social followings than it is to market themselves.

Plus, they know that your personal recommendation about their products means a lot than them advertising, and they'll sell more if they can incentivize you to make that recommendation!

Think of it this way.

You recommend a good restaurant to a friend. Your friend dines at that restaurant spending $100 on himself and his family there. The restaurant, if they participated in an affiliate marketing campaign would send you a percentage, say 20%.

So that would be $20 in your pocket.

The same thing happens online, only it's all tracked through affiliate networks!

You send a friend (AKA a lead) to a company. Your lead buys. You get paid!

Here are a couple typical affiliate marketing scenarios that you'll see time and time again online:

1. You recommend a TV on Amazon.com, using a special link. If somebody actually clicks that link and buys the TV you get paid.
2. You can recommend an ebook for sale on ClickBank.com, and if someone buys it, you get paid.
3. You recommend the audiobook service, Audible.com, to a friend on Facebook. Your friend signs up for their trial program and you make $25.

Best yet, you don't need to worry about any of the tracking! Affiliate networks take care of all that for you, and you just collect a check!

There are lots of affiliate networks online that'll let you promote stuff for a commission, but the one that we like the best is ClickBank.

Aside from offering commissions up to 75% of the purchase price, ClickBank features some of the best digital products in the world that solve real world, every day problems! It's also very reliable about paying affiliates their commissions on time, like clockwork.

Getting Started on ClickBank

For those of you who don't know anything about ClickBank.com, it's one of the world's leading digital product marketplaces and one of the oldest. You'll find ebooks, video courses, membership sites, etc. on there. Every once in a while, you'll also see physical products there as well.

The true power of ClickBank is that it brings affiliates and product owners together. People who want to sell their ebooks list them for sale in ClickBank. Affiliates like us can help promote those ebooks. ClickBank processes the sale and make sure everyone is paid.

It's a beautiful model, and it works very well.

As an affiliate, commissions are usually 50-75% of the total product price. Each product has its own affiliate link you use in conjunction with your ClickBank account that tracks clicks and sales.

You also get bi-weekly or weekly payments, so you can absolutely treat it like a paycheck from a job! That's actually how I made the transition when I started out.

As soon as my weekly check from ClickBank passed that of my day job for three months, I quit :0) (Of course, I didn't want to quit too early...)

Now, if you already have a ClickBank account, awesome! If you're new to affiliate marketing and ClickBank, the first step is to sign up for a ClickBank account. There is no charge to open an affiliate account.

What to Promote from ClickBank

Inside ClickBank, there are tens of thousands of different products that you can promote, in almost every niche or category you can imagine...

What to promote? How do I find people who will buy these products? How do I know that this one will convert?

There are lots and lots of questions that you'll be asking yourself as you start getting into ClickBank... The most helpful advice I can share though is this: Choose a niche that you're interested in.

The most successful marketers in the world find something that they're passionate about, and they build their entire list around that one topic.

The beautiful thing about ClickBank is you can find 10 or 12 different things you can sell to your audience without having to create any of them!

What we do in niches is we find something we enjoy, like woodworking. To find all of the products on woodworking, go to the ClickBank marketplace. Sign into your account and look for the link labeled Marketplace in the menu at the top of the page.

Inside the marketplace, on the left side, you can start filtering through categories.

Unfortunately, woodworking products are scattered all around ClickBank, so we're going to use the search box. For whatever reason, a lot of product owners put their products in categories that don't make sense, like they might put the woodworking product in Health or Business or somewhere else. So when you start going through a category or subcategory looking for products to promote, just keep in mind that you'll have to wade through lots of miscategorized products.

When you enter in your search, like 'wood,' you'll get some pretty crazy results. The default search doesn't sort very well – and it certainly doesn't tell us how well a product is selling!

So, we're going to click on 'Advanced Search.'

From there, you'll see the advanced search screen.

There are two things that you'll want to enter:

1. The search keyword (of course!)
2. Filter for a Gravity Score of above 20

The Gravity score in ClickBank is an algorithmic number, meaning it's a score that's given to a product based on how many sales are made, how many affiliates are successfully promoting, and how many refunds the product owner is getting.

There are probably lots of other variables associated with the Gravity score but the simple explanation is the higher the better. Exactly how the gravity is calculated is a secret that ClickBank won't reveal. It does seem like the number of affiliates who have made a sale of the product counts for a lot, so sometimes there is a product with a low gravity that has made a decent number of sales, but very few of the sales were made by affiliates.

I generally filter out all the products that have a Gravity score below 20. If something is below 20, that means that it's not really a good fit for our email list – the volume of sales are too low and the sales copy hasn't been fully tested yet.

In getting back to the woodworking example, after we filter based on gravity, we get a list of products that we can promote…

Now, of the products that are there – one of them isn't a fit… It's a muscle-building offer it looks like, so we'll omit that one.

We do need some more depth though for our affiliate sequence, so we're going to search for some different products. So we might search for a related word like 'plans.'

Not all of these are going to be a fit, but it's reasonable to assume that if someone is looking for woodworking projects, they might be interested in building a shed or a boat too!

Now, put together a list of 10 or 12 affiliate products that you want to promote, and get your affiliate link for each one of those products.

Getting Your Affiliate Link

To get your affiliate link, go to any product that's in ClickBank and hit the button that says "Promote."

Then, enter in your ClickBank ID and optionally, a tracking ID in the screen that pops up. (If you don't understand tracking Ids, don't worry, just leave that blank for now.)

From there, you'll get your affiliate link, which ClickBank calls a hoplink.

That's the link that you'll use in your email promotions, so make sure to keep it safe. Whenever, where ever you want to promote the affiliate product, you'll use that link.

NOTE: Inside Scriptly, we take care of finding the best affiliate products for you, by niche. Plus, we make it super easy to get your affiliate links! Just fill in a short form and we'll create 45+ days worth of email copy for you to use! Go here to get started: **scriptly.org**

What to Do With Your Affiliate Links

Now you know which products you're going to promote, and you have your affiliate links... What's next?

Well, the next thing that you're going to need to do is write emails promoting your affiliate products to your list!

Normally, we set these up inside that autoresponder series of our email marketing platform. That way when someone opts-in, they go through a promotional sequence that's already all set up from beginning to end.

Typically, we'll set up somewhere between 10 to 12 products, with anywhere between 3 and 5 emails promoting each product. That gives almost 2 full months of marketing, all done for you.

Scriptly handles all of the emails for you, and follows this process for promoting products: It sends 3-4 emails promoting product 1 on consecutive days, then three days later it does the same thing with product 2, and so on.

Once someone opts-in to our list, they go from product promotion to product promotion, following a systematic process. You can add bonding emails in the middle, by sending links to Youtube videos or blog posts.

At the end of the day though, we want someone to opt-in and buy some of the affiliate products, so we can get paid!

And, to get the affiliate autoresponders all done for you, make sure to check out Scriptly at **scriptly.org**.

Conclusion

There you have it, some of my best stuff on conversion, or more simply put, how to sell more stuff online.

Of course, I can't possibly put everything there is to know about Internet marketing in one book, so I have focused on the main ways we make sales in our business: email marketing, video sales letters, webinars, and strategy sessions.

There are many other things you can do to get traffic and make sales online, but if you focus on what we cover here, you will be off to a great start and well ahead of 80% of your competition.

I hope you've enjoyed reading this book and learned from it, but more importantly, I hope you take action and implement what it teaches. After all, just reading about sales copy and autoresponders and so on won't do anything for your business until you act on what you've learned.

To schedule a call for a customized action plan for your business, go to:

http://doneforyou.com/schedule/

And finally, come check out our software, Scriptly.org, Curately.org, and TimeSlots.org; see the About the Author page for more details.

ABOUT THE AUTHOR

Jason Drohn is an Erie, PA-based entrepreneur and the creator of several software solutions to save you time and make your business more efficient, including:

Scriptly.org

Generates email sequences and other marketing materials and builds your landing pages for many purposes.

Statly.org

Analytics and sales funnel tracking platform to give you more insight into the traffic that's hitting your site and the sales channels that are driving revenue.

Askly.org

Survey and quiz platform created to help business owners get better insight into what their prospects and customers want from them, for development and marketing.

Convertly.org

Email marketing software for businesses and website owners, delivering email marketing and automation that just works…

Curately.org

Curates content for your website in minutes.

TimeSlots.org

Easy scheduling, especially for coaching and other high-ticket services.

He is also the founder of **DoneForYou.com**, which creates a variety of custom marketing solutions for companies in many different niches and industries. If you would like to work with him and his team, visit DoneForYou.com.

www.ingramcontent.com/pod-product-compliance
Lightning Source LLC
Chambersburg PA
CBHW070924210326
41520CB00021B/6796